FOLLOWING JESUS

AT HOME

AT WORK

IN ALL OF LIFE

Chris J. Fenner

A GUIDEBOOK TO EXPERIENCE A
CLOSE WALK WITH JESUS

FOLLOWING JESUS

AT HOME

AT WORK

IN ALL OF LIFE

His Victory Publishing

Roseville, CA

Chris J. Fenner

HVP

His Victory Publishing, Roseville, CA

"Following Jesus in the Details of Life" hardcover edition, May 2017
"Following Jesus at Home, at Work, in all of Life" paperback edition,
May 2019
Updated, May 2023

HIS VICTORY PUBLISHING

Roseville, CA

http://www.chrisjfenner.com/

International Standard Book Number

978-0-9815419-5-2

Acknowledgments

Many people were part of my coming to know the Lord and my learning to follow Jesus in all of life—the following are those who have been particularly precious to me:

my mother, Vera May Blay, who was a living example of following Jesus;

my friend and coworker Sheryl Garret, who witnessed to me in a silent yet profound way as he lived a life of "following Jesus at home, at work, in all of life" even as his wife suffered and died through a long battle with cancer;

the godly men in Santa Barbara, California, who encouraged me during the two-year sabbatical from my career in the oil industry as I sought the Lord and His will for my life—especially Al Phau, who God used in a powerful way to direct me back to work;

Steve Wetch, Luiz Bensimon, Max Lewis, Janet Pool, Wendy Landry, Susan Martin, and Cassandra Massee, who joined with me in prayer, fellowship and Bible Study at Imodco Inc. in Agoura Hills, California;

Kevin McCaffery, Bill Kramer, Doug Milliken, Scott Bailey, Ken Ellsworth, Tim Cleary—longtime members of a men's small group in Westlake Village, California—now lifetime friends;

Pastor Gordy Duncan, Tori Yamada, Len Sunukian, Willett Tuitele, Dan Morgan, Gail Irwin, Chris Steffen—faithful pray-ers for God's glory;

Chris Hartman, Matt Svoboda, John Gommel, Danny Ayala, Martin Fuentes, and the other men and women at the SBM companies in Houston, who regularly met together for Bible study, fellowship and prayer;

Pastor Steve Bass, Travis Brunner, Charlie Crawford, Edward Sneider, Mike Kelly, Ron Gere, Martin Fuentes—men who helped me refine this guidebook by their participation in Saturday morning study groups;

Sharon Tice and Tori Yamada—wonderful and faithful prayer partners and prayer warriors, who I could always turn to for intercessory prayer;

most of all—in all things and through all things—my wife, Diana.

Reaction From Participants

Here are some reactions from participants in groups that have used the *Following Jesus* guidebook.

Charlie Crawford: "God spoke to me through His Word. Here was a Bible study that drew me in first thing daily. I loved writing how God spoke to me and sharing with my group on Saturday mornings. Thanks, Chris!"

Martin Fuentes: "The more I study this book the more God becomes real in my life and gives my spirit strength; my faith grows and my love for others expands. My love for my wife has been renewed through this guidebook and I am feeling something special for her like when we first met."

Charlie Matcek: "The *Following Jesus* guidebook made me focus on what was most important in my life—my faith in God—during a time when my life had many competing priorities. The selected Bible verses and associated questions made me dig deep to uncover my beliefs. This produced rich discussions in the weekly group meetings that led to application of those beliefs to my life situation. How powerful and encouraging this was!"

John Songu: "I have gained tremendous spiritual benefit from studying *Following Jesus*. The sections contain valuable Biblical information that I will always use."

Jennifer Stuckey: The *Following Jesus* guidebook is unique in that it allows the participant to be absorbed in particular scriptures pertaining to the topic of the week. The reflection questions and challenges give great insight into the various aspects of knowing, abiding and achieving victory in Jesus. This guidebook involved me in an opportunity to deepen my faith journey as I rediscovered the unique blessings of the Christian life. The experience was personal and intimate drawing me closer to the Savior."

Diana Fenner: "God spoke to me through the scriptures in *Following Jesus* and this helped me to come to know myself and to change the things God wanted me to change so that I joyfully and willingly obey Him."

Betty Schwarz: "If I have a chance to go through this guidebook again, I most certainly will do so."

Dedication

Following Jesus at Home, at Work, in all of Life is dedicated to the 72% of Christian men and women who are unable to integrate their faith into their work lives.

The Barna Group's 2018 report *Christians at Work* notes that only 28% of Christians in the work place are *Faith-work Integrators*. That is to say, Christians who try to live out their faith at work.

Table of Contents

Preface

I came to know our Lord Jesus Christ in midlife and spent two years away from my career in the oil industry seeking to find a different path of life that I thought the Lord was leading me to. At the end of these two years, however, it became clear I was to return to my previous type of work, but now in His service.

As I started this new, and renewed, phase of life, the question came to my mind, "Okay, I am now a Christian. How am I supposed to behave?" In this I sought the Lord, and over a three-month period the writing for *Knowing Him* (see the opening page of Part 1) came to me, which became an outline for my daily walk with Jesus.

Over the next five years, I was led by the Lord to develop this single writing into a practical guidebook that Christians could use to learn how to live for the Lord in all of life—including the workplace. And it was through my participation with several different groups over the next twenty years that ***Following Jesus at Home, at Work, in all of Life*** emerged in its final form. The emphasis is on following Jesus at work**; however, this is only possible if it is integrated with following Jesus at home and in all of life.

The focus of this guidebook is God's Word, and through the meditation on twenty-six topics—by daily reading of short passages of the Bible—God will lead you, speak to your heart, and reveal His presence to you in practical ways.

Chris J. Fenner
April 2019

** **Work** is used in the broad sense of those activities that are the primary focus of our weekdays including: paid employment, volunteer work, vocational work, and homemaker work.

How To Use This Guidebook

Imagine your favorite recent President of the United States asked you to spend ten minutes with him every day, at which time he would give you his undivided attention, listen attentively to you, and impart his wisdom to you on topics that were dearest to your heart. For most people, such a privilege would be a huge honor and joy they would look forward to with great anticipation every day.

This is just a small illustration of how our daily devotional time with our Lord should be, but instead of meeting with the President of the United States we meet with the King of kings, the Lord of lords, the Lord God Almighty. He, even more so, gives us His undivided attention and imparts His wisdom to us for that day that is infinitely beyond the wisdom of any man. Shame on us that we are not excited about each moment in His presence, as we often prefer to forgo time with the Creator and Sustainer of all things to do something that appears to be a priority to us, but has no lasting importance!

This guidebook is a tool to help you build the wonderful discipline of spending time with our Lord in a meaningful way as described above. The daily Bible readings take no more than five minutes to read, so even if you are hard pressed for time the devotional of Bible reading and prayer can be completed in ten minutes. And what a blessed ten minutes this will be—ten minutes that will change your life!

```
┌─────────────────────────────────────────────────────┐
│                      Caution                         │
│  Replacing the daily readings and time of prayer     │
│  with a once-a-week reading of all the scriptures    │
│  not only limits the opportunity to meditate on the  │
│  topic, but it also limits the opportunity for God   │
│  to lead you, speak to you, and to providentially    │
│  work in your life..                                 │
└─────────────────────────────────────────────────────┘
```

There is benefit in using this as a personal guidebook. The benefit is greatly enhanced, however, with weekly small group meetings.

Finally, it is important to keep this guidebook as a continuous activity through the twenty-six weeks. Even if you, or the whole group, are unable to meet—because of holidays, vacations or any other reason—keep meeting with God. He is always there and wants to meet with you every day.

The Voice of the Lord

In the heading to each week's journal pages you will see the sentence, "Make notes about your journey with Jesus this week; for example, how He led you; how He spoke to you...." The key is to remember that our Lord wants to have a relationship and conversation with each of His followers and His "voice" may come to us in many different ways and at unexpected times.

The following prose, delighting in the many ways the Lord speaks to us, may help you to understand the diverse ways that our Lord speaks to His children.

YOUR VOICE

I delight, O Lord, in your voice!

You speak to us through the scriptures from Genesis to Malachi, from Matthew to Revelation, that we may know You more, that we may love You more (see Psalm 119:105).

You speak to us through Your Spirit, made possible by Jesus dying for our sins, that we may know You more, that we may love You more (see John 7:38).

You speak to us through Your creation: the heavens, even the highest heavens, and the earth with all its beauty, that we may know You more, that we may love You more (see Isaiah 6:3b).

You speak to us in answer to our prayers, that we may know You more, that we may love You more (see 1 John 5:14).

You speak to us through Your faithful servants, both those with us and the legacies of those with You, that we may know You more, that we may love You more (see Ephesians 4:11).

You speak to us through fellowship with other believers in many diverse and surprising ways, that we may know You more, that we may love You more (see Hebrews 10:24).

You speak to us through the details of life and the wonderful 'coincidences' that can only come from You, that we may know You more, that we may love You more (see 2 Corinthians 9:8).

You speak to us through the events of each day7: the joys, the sorrows; the victories, the defeats, that we may know You more, that we may love You more (see Romans 8:28).

You speak to us, at times, through visions and dreams to fulfill Your purposes, that we may know You more, that we may love You more (see Acts 2:17b).

I delight, O Lord, in your voice! Yes, even to hear You speak (see 1 Samuel 3:9b).

Weekly Meeting Format

If possible, leadership of the weekly meetings should rotate through the group members.

As leader of the group, commit to being a role model for daily meeting with our Lord in the assigned scriptures and in prayer; and to be willing to share your joys and despairs, and your breakthroughs and setbacks on the pilgrimage of following Jesus at home, at work, in all of life.

Each chapter is formatted to provide an easy to follow outline for the group discussions, with additional time for prayer added as agreed by the group. Also it will quickly become evident that the most benefit is obtained by starting the meeting with an opening prayer then sharing how the Lord has worked in each group member's life during the previous week.

Week 1: Introduction

Do all things work together in your life so that you are able to fulfill your responsibilities and the desires of your heart without worry or distress?

> *And we know that in all things God works for the good of those who love him, who have been called according to his purpose* (Romans 8:28).

Are the fruit of the Spirit manifest in your life such that they are evident to other people?

> *But the fruit of the Spirit is love, joy, peace, patience, kindness, goodness, faithfulness, gentleness and self-control (Galatians 5:22-23a).*

Do you walk in the fullness of Christ with His gifts manifest in your life through the grace of God?

> *But to each one of us grace has been given as Christ apportioned it* (Ephesians 4:7).

Do you know our Savior so intimately that His purpose and your purpose in life are one?

> *I have made you known to them, and will continue to make you known in order that the love you have for me may be in them and that I myself may be in them* (John 17:26, Jesus' prayer for all believers).

Is your life a continual witness to the lost and to the saved?

> *For we are to God the aroma of Christ among those who are being saved and those who are perishing* (2 Corinthians 2:15).

The gospel of Jesus Christ promises an answer of, "Yes!" to these questions. Yet we are so often mired in the ways of the world, saved yet lost to many of the promises of our Savior.

After His resurrection, Jesus gave His disciples what we call today the Great Commission: *"Therefore go and make disciples..."* (Matthew 28:19a). He said this because He knew for God's will to be done in our lives, and for the fullness of the good news to be manifest in our lives, we must move beyond knowing Him merely as our Savior. He knew we would need to be His true followers—His disciples.

Consequently, to get out of the mire of this world, we must become true disciples of Jesus Christ. And to become true disciples, we must allow Jesus to lead us from a life that follows the ways of the world to a life where the Spirit of God fills us so that we may fulfill His purpose for us. This is the promise of Jesus when he tells us, "*If you love me, you will obey what I command. And I will ask the Father, and he will give you another Counselor to be with you forever—the Spirit of truth...*" (John 14:15-17a).

But how can this become a meaningful reality in our lives?

Five books of the Bible, Exodus through Joshua, are devoted to the story of the Israelites' journey out of captivity into the Promised Land. This story contains important parallels for us today as we also make a journey from being captive to the ways of the world to the "promised land" of a life filled with the presence of Jesus.

Some key points of the story of the Israelites' journey are as follows:

† They were God's chosen people while they were still in captivity in Egypt.

† God led them to the Promised Land by the way of the desert to test their hearts.

† After the initial excitement of leaving captivity, they quickly yearned for their old way of life.

† When it came time to enter the Promised Land, many were afraid, and they turned aside only to wander in the desert.

† As they trusted wholeheartedly in God, so the time came to enter the Promised Land, but this involved many battles.

† Finally, God's promise of living in a land filled with "milk and honey" was fulfilled.

Once we accept Jesus Christ, we too are God's chosen people, but like the Israelites, we are still in captivity—captive to the ways of the world (see 1 Peter 2:9). And we are called out of this "captivity" to follow Jesus to the "promised land" of a life filled with His presence and marked by the fruit of the Spirit (see Galatians 5:22-23). Also the road to this "promised land" passes through a desert, where God tests our hearts, and it is in this suffering we break free from our old natures and learn to abide in Him.

Also the way into the "promised land" of a Spirit-filled life is not easy, but it is a fight—a fight that only Jesus can win. The enemy is the great deceiver who wants us to stay captive to the ways of the world.

But thanks be to God! He gives us the victory through our Lord Jesus Christ (1 Corinthians 15:57).

This then is the foundation of *Following Jesus: at Home, at Work, in all of Life*: to abide in the Lord, to know the indwelling Holy Spirit, to find peace and joy, and to be a light in a world of darkness.

Each person's journey to this "promised land" is different, but the promise of the abundant life where the "streams of living water will flow from within" is the same (see John 7:38).

The first part of *Following Jesus* is *Knowing Him* which covers the basic principles of living a Christian life.

The second part is the journey across the desert where God tests our hearts as we learn to *Abide In Him*.

Finally, *His Victory* covers the battle to enter the "promised land" where Jesus gains full control of our lives so that we can know His marvelous blessings: the fruit of the Spirit, the gifts of the Spirit that have been apportioned to us, the fullness of God's grace, and a desire to serve only Him.

Challenge for This Week

It is important to establish a daily routine for Bible reading and prayer; therefore, this is the main challenge for the first week. Read the assigned daily Bible passage included in this guidebook accompanied by a time of prayer. And remember, you are entering into the presence of our heavenly Father, the Lord God Almighty, for a one-on-one conversation with Him every day! He gives you His time and is waiting for you. How can we not make this a priority and a joyful privilege?

Daily Bible Readings for Week 1

Day 1-3: The Israelites' Journey

Day 1, read Exodus 3:1-10 (A chosen people)

Key verse: *"So I have come down to rescue [my people] from the hand of the Egyptians and to bring them up out of that land into a good and spacious land, a land flowing with milk and honey..."* (v. 8a).

Day 2, read Exodus 13:17-22 (Led by the Spirit)

Key verse: *By day the LORD went ahead of them in a pillar of cloud to guide them on their way and by night in a pillar of fire to give them light, so that they could travel by day or night* (v. 21).

Day 3, read Joshua 23:1-16 (To the Promised Land)

Key *verse*: *"You know with all your heart and soul that not one of all the good promises the LORD your God gave you has failed. Every promise has been fulfilled..."* (v. 14b).

Day 4-6 Our Journey

Day 4, read 1 Peter 2:4-12 (A chosen people)

Key verse: *But you are a chosen people, a royal priesthood, a holy nation, a people belonging to God, that you may declare the praises of him who called you out of darkness into his wonderful light* (v. 9).

Day 5, read John 16:5-16 (Led by the Spirit)

Key verse: *"But when he, the Spirit of truth, comes, he will guide you into all truth"* (v.13a).

Day 6, read Galatians 5:16-26 (To the "promised land")

Key verse: *But the fruit of the Spirit is love, joy, peace, patience, kindness, goodness, faithfulness, gentleness, and self-control* (vv. 22-23a).

Week 1 Journal

Make notes about your journey with Jesus this week; for example, how He led you; how He spoke to you (see *Your Voice* on page 4); how God worked providentially in your circumstances; breakthroughs and setbacks.

....

....

....

....

Note: there is additional journal space at the end of the guidebook.

Part I: Knowing Him

May I have faith to know You are always present to guide me at home, at work, in all of life.

May I have hope to know that my trust in You will not be disappointed.

May I have love towards all people I meet this day.

May I remember that it is not for me to direct my own steps, but to follow Your way.

May I remember that it is not for me to seek power over others, but to serve others.

May I remember that it is not for me to worry about tomorrow, but sufficient to do Your will this day.

May I know the peace and confidence that comes from following Your way.

May I know the joy that springs from this peace as I see You move in the lives of those who love You.

May I know that all of this is possible as I pray and give praise in all things.

Amen.

This prayer is to remind us of the principles of Christian living; consequently, each verse is a signpost to a greater truth in God's Word, and these are the topics for the next nine weeks.

Reminder

For this guidebook to help you have an intimate, living relationship with our Lord and Savior Jesus Christ, it is important to establish the discipline of meeting with Him <u>daily</u> in His Word and prayer.

Week 2: Faith

May I have faith to know You are always present to guide me at home, at work, in all of life.

The meaning of faith has become diluted in our society as there has been a movement away from the true God. The meaning of Christian faith is unchanging, however, as summarized in the Great Commandment: "*Love the Lord your God with all your heart and with all your soul and with all your mind*" (Matthew 22:37b). It is by loving the Lord in the fullness of the Great Commandment that His Presence, the Holy Spirit, guides us in all truth.

> There is a faith of insight, a faith of desire, a faith of trust in the truth of the word, and a faith of personal acceptance. There is a faith of love that embraces, a faith of will that holds fast, and a faith of sacrifice that gives up everything, and a faith of despair that abandons all hope in self, and a faith of rest that waits on God alone. This is all included in the faith of a true heart, the fullness of faith, in which the whole being surrenders and lets go all, and yields itself to God to do His work. In fullness of faith lets us draw near.
>
> *Andrew Murray* [1]

I have found that our walk with the Lord is more one of deletion than addition. The Lord does not want to add greater burdens to our lives as we seek and strive to do His work; rather, He wants to simplify our lives so that we release everything related to our old, worldly natures and trust only in Him. This simplicity is expressed beautifully in Genesis 5:24 where the writer tells us, "*Enoch walked with God*". And the same need for this simple walk with God came to me as I struggled to live the life God had called me to live.

THE WIND OF THE SPIRIT

The ship *My Lord God Almighty* is ready, but the anchor is still set and the sails are still furled—even though the fair wind of the Spirit is blowing—for I am still in the waters of struggling faith trying to get to the ship.

The ship *My Lord God Almighty* is ready, but the anchor is still set and the sails are still furled—even though the fair wind of the Spirit is blowing—for I am still in the waters of clinging faith holding onto the side of the ship.

The ship *My Lord God Almighty* is ready with the anchor raised and the sails unfurled, and the fair wind of the Spirit is blowing. Now resting faith has brought me into the ship ready to embark on the journey of life for His glory.

Reflection and Discussion

Review the author's experience above and think about situations where your faith is strong and where your faith is still fragile?

Are you able to integrate your faith into your work life? If so how is this manifested?

Challenge for This Week

This week pray that God may reveal to you the things you are withholding from Him; that is to say, where you have struggling faith or clinging faith.

Memory Verse

Love the Lord your God with all your heart and with all your soul and with all your mind (Matthew 22:37).

Daily Bible Readings for Week 2

Day 1, read Genesis 22:1-14

Key verse: *So Abraham called that place The Lord Will Provide. And to this day it is said, "On the mountain of the Lord it will be provided"* (v. 14).

Day 2, read Matthew 14:22-36

Key verse: *Immediately Jesus reached out his hand and caught him. "You of little faith," he said, "why did you doubt?"* (v. 31).

Day 3, read John 14:1-14

Key verse: *"I tell you the truth, anyone who has faith in me will do what I have been doing. He will do even greater things than these, because I am going to the Father"* (v. 12).

Day 4, read Romans 1:8-17

Key verse: *For in the gospel a righteousness from God is revealed, a righteousness that is by faith from first to last, just as it is written: "The righteous will live by faith"* (v. 17).

Day 5, read 2 Corinthians 5:1-10

Key verse: *We live by faith, not by sight* (v. 7).

Day 6, read Hebrews 11:1-13

Key verse: *Now faith is being sure of what we hope for and certain of what we do not see* (v. 1).

Week 2 Journal

Make notes about your journey with Jesus this week; for example, how He led you; how He spoke to you (see *Your Voice* on page 4); how God worked providentially in your circumstances; breakthroughs and setbacks.

Note: there is additional journal space at the end of the guidebook.

Week 3: Hope

May I have hope to know that my trust in You will not be disappointed.

Many people are frustrated because either they cannot find a true sense of hope and purpose in their lives, or they cannot fulfill the purpose they have found. Moreover, if we trust only in our own efforts, this frustration will continue, but the Lord promises fulfillment when He tells us, *"Those who hope in me will not be disappointed"* (Isaiah 49:23b).

> Thus, when a person is newly born of the Spirit, his grasp of God's purpose for him is usually very limited and his experience is limited in proportion. But as the Holy Spirit enlightens the eyes of his heart, vistas begin to open up before him of which at first he had scarcely even dreamed. He begins to see and know the hope of God's calling, the riches of God's inheritance and the greatness of God's power.
>
> *John R. W. Stott* [2]

The Lord made Abraham wait for twenty-five years for the promised son to be born. The Lord allowed Joseph to wallow in a prison for over a decade before the time was right for him to become second only to Pharaoh in Egypt. Moses fled to the desolate parts of Midian when his attempt to do God's will failed, and then the Lord left him there for forty years. Why the delay in using these great men of the Bible? So that they would learn to rely only on Him and that their only hope was in Him. And so it is today. The Lord cannot use us until we shed any hope in ourselves.

IN THIS I CAN REJOICE

In this I can rejoice!
I have hope in the Lord for today.
He will guide me and guard me through the
difficulties.

In this I can rejoice!
I have hope in the Lord for tomorrow.
He will fulfill His purpose for me.

In this I can rejoice!
I have hope in the Lord for eternity.
He will lead me home to the place He has prepared.

In this I can rejoice!

Reflection and Discussion

What are your goals in life, and what provides you with hope and a sense of purpose?

What part do you think God has in bringing hope and a sense of purpose to your life at work?

Challenge for This Week

This week pray for a deeper understanding of how your relationship with Jesus Christ is related to your purpose in life.

Memory Verse

"For I know the plans I have for you," declares the Lord, *"plans to prosper you and not to harm you, plans to give you hope and a future"* (Jeremiah 29:11).

Daily Bible Readings for Week 3

Day 1, read Psalm 62:1-8

Key verse: *Find rest, O my soul, in God alone; my hope comes from him* (v. 5).

Day 2, read Proverbs 16:3, 19:21, 20:24, 23:17 and 18

Key verse: *Many are the plans in a man's heart, but it is the* Lord's *purpose that prevails* (Proverbs 19:21).

Day 3, Jeremiah 29:4-14

Key verse: *"For I know the plans I have for you," declares the* Lord, *"plans to prosper you and not to harm you, plans to give you hope and a future"* (v. 11).

Day 4, read Hebrews 6:13-20

Key verse: *We have this hope as an anchor for the soul, firm and secure* (v. 19a).

Day 5, read Hebrews 10:19-25

Key verse: *Let us hold unswervingly to the hope we profess, for he who promised is faithful* (v. 23).

Day 6, read 1 Peter 1:13-21

Key verse: *Therefore, prepare your minds for action; be self-controlled; set your hope fully on the grace to be given you when Jesus Christ is revealed* (v. 13).

Week 3 Journal

Make notes about your journey with Jesus this week; for example, how He led you; how He spoke to you (see *Your Voice* on page 4); how God worked providentially in your circumstances; breakthroughs and setbacks

Note: there is additional journal space at the end of the guidebook.

Week 4: Love

May I have love toward all people I meet this day.

In 1 Corinthians 13, Paul shows us *"the most excellent way"*—the way of love—which is as applicable today as it was to the Corinthians almost two thousand years ago. Starting at the fourth verse of this chapter, Paul defines the meaning of love: *Love is patient, love is kind. It does not envy, it does not boast, it is not proud. It is not rude, it is not self-seeking, it is not easily angered, it keeps no record of wrongs. Love does not delight in evil but rejoices with the truth. It always protects, always trusts, always hopes, always perseveres* (1 Corinthians 13:4-7).

> So for all of us, it doesn't matter what we are doing or where we are as long as we remember that we belong to him, that we are his, that we are in love with him. The means he gives us, whether we are working for the rich or we are working for the poor, whether we are working with high-class people or low-class people, it makes no difference; but how much love we are putting into the work we do is what matters.
>
> *Mother Teresa* [3]

It is often when we stumble and fall that we learn the most. This has certainly been true for me, and in one of these times of failure—when my actions grieved a good friend and pastor who had helped me through a most difficult period in my walk with the Lord—I realized that Jesus did not have all of my life, and the part that He did not have was still self-centered and unloving. These words came to me and captured what I still had yet to learn.

LOVE IS...

Love is Jesus living in me.

Jesus is love and His love is alive in me if I truly love Him. Therefore if I say, "I love Jesus," yet I do not love others I deceive myself and the truth is not in me.

If I love little it is because I love Jesus little.

If I love much it is because I love Jesus much.
Love is Jesus living in me.
In this I can rejoice!

Reflection and Discussion

Rate yourself on a scale of 1 to 10 against the definition of love described in Paul's letter to the Corinthians (see below).

Is there a difference between how you are able to love others at work and in the rest of lie?

Love...

is patient ( )	keeps no record of wrongs ( )
is kind ( )	does not delight in evil ( )
does not envy ( )	rejoices with the truth ( )
does not boast ( )	always protect ( )
is not proud ( )	always trust ( )
is not rude ( )	always hope ( )
is not self-seeking ( )	always persevere ( )
is not easily angered ( )	

Challenge for This Week

In prayer, seek God for more of His presence and His love.

Memory Verse

Live a life of love, just as Christ loved us and gave himself up for us as a fragrant offering and sacrifice to God (Ephesians 5:2).

Daily Bible Readings for Week 4

Day 1, read Proverbs 3:1-4

Key verse: *Let love and faithfulness never leave you; bind them around your neck, write them on the tablet of your heart* (v. 3).

Day 2, read Mark 12:28-34

Key verse: *"The second is this: 'Love your neighbor as yourself.' There is no commandment greater than these"* (v. 31).

Day 3, read Luke 6:27-36

Key verse: *"Do to others as you would have them do to you"* (v. 31).

Day 4, read 1 Corinthians 13:1-13

Key verse: *And now these three remain: faith, hope and love. But the greatest of these is love* (v. 13).

Day 5, read Ephesians 5:1-21

Key verse: *... and live a life of love, just as Christ loved us and gave himself up for us as a fragrant offering and sacrifice to God* (v. 2).

Day 6, read 1 John 4:7-21

Key verse: *Dear friends, let us love one another, for love comes from God. Everyone who loves has been born of God and knows God* (v. 7).

Week 4 Journal

Make notes about your journey with Jesus this week; for example, how He led you; how He spoke to you (see *Your Voice* on page 4); how God worked providentially in your circumstances; breakthroughs and setbacks.

Note: there is additional journal space at the end of the guidebook.

Week 5: God's Way

May I remember that it is not for me to direct my own steps, but to follow Your way.

Life can be compared to walking through a maze as each day, and often each hour of each day, we must make decisions. These may be small decisions, such as how we respond to criticism from another person, or major decisions that determine the direction of our lives, a company, or an organization. But regardless of the magnitude of the decision, the real decision is always the same: whether we will follow God's way or our own way.

Jeremiah said, *"I know, O Lord, that a man's life is not his own; it is not for man to direct his steps"* (Jeremiah 10:23).

> [If] we behold Jesus Christ going on before step by step, we shall not go astray. But if we worry about the dangers that beset us, if we gaze at the road instead of at him who goes before, we are already straying from the path. For he is himself the way, the narrow way and the narrow gate. He, and he alone, is our journey's end.
>
> *Dietrich Bonhoeffer* [4]

I had followed the Lord as faithfully as I could for over twelve years when I entered a period of great trial. The vision I had from the Lord was as far as ever from being fulfilled. Some of the long term financial decisions my wife and I had made, so that we could be ready to be used by the Lord, appeared to have been misguided. To top it off, the transmissions on both of our automobiles went out within three days of each other!

As the trials deepened I got caught in a dangerous inner conflict like the motions of a crosscut saw: one day remaining faithful to my calling and the next day full of fear, running to catch up with the ways of the world. At the height of my distress I was scheduled to be an evangelism volunteer at a Promise Keepers event, but when I was on the field to pray for others the Lord placed on my heart to take off my EV badge and turn to another volunteer for prayer. Before this period of trial came to a close I had to realize that my Lord needed to be Lord of all regardless of my immediate circumstances.

THY WILL, O LORD

Thy will, O Lord, not mine.

Thy way, O Lord, not mine.

Thy time, O Lord, not mine.

Thy all, O Lord, not mine.

Reflection and Discussion

To what extent do you think that God is concerned about the details of our lives: at home, at work, in all of life?

Have you sensed the providential hand of God working in the details of your work life so that you area able to carry out your responsibilities more effectively?

Challenge for This Week

Think about those parts of your life that still follow the world's ways and in prayer seek the Lord's guidance about how you can more fully follow His ways.

Memory Verse

Then he said to them all: "If anyone would come after me, he must deny himself and take up his cross daily and follow me" (Luke 9:23).

Daily Bible Readings for Week 5

Day 1, read Deuteronomy 10:12-22

Key verse: *And now, O Israel, what does the LORD your God ask of you but to fear the LORD your God, to walk in all his ways, to love him, to serve the LORD your God with all your heart and with all your soul...* (v. 12).

Day 2, read Isaiah 42:10-17

Key verse: *I will lead the blind by ways they have not known, along unfamiliar paths I will guide them...* (v. 16a).

Day 3, read Luke 9:18-27

Key verse: *Then he said to them all: "If anyone would come after me, he must deny himself and take up his cross daily and follow me"* (v. 23).

Day 4, read John 12:20-36

Key verse: *"Whoever serves me must follow me; and where I am, my servant also will be. My father will honor the one who serves me"* (v. 26).

Day 5, read 1 Peter 2:13-25

Key verse: *To this you were called, because Christ suffered for you, leaving you an example, that you should follow in his steps* (v. 21).

Day 6, read 1 John 2:1-11

Key verse: *Whoever claims to live in him must walk as Jesus did* (v. 6).

Week 5 Journal

Make notes about your journey with Jesus this week; for example, how He led you; how He spoke to you (see *Your Voice* on page 4); how God worked providentially in your circumstances; breakthroughs and setbacks.

Note: there is additional journal space at the end of the guidebook.

Week 6: Serving Others

May I remember that it is not for me to seek power over others,
but to serve others.

When some of Christ's disciples selfishly sought to gain power and authority in His kingdom, He said to them, *"Whoever wants to become great among you must be your servant, and whoever wants to be first must be your slave—just as the Son of Man did not come to be served, but to serve, and to give his life as a ransom for many"* (Matthew 20:26-28).

As Christians we are similarly called to serve others rather than to seek power over others.

> According to faith we are in need of nothing, and have an abundance; according to love we are servants of all. By faith we receive blessings from above, from God; through love we give them out below, to our neighbor. Even as Christ in his divinity stood in need of nothing, but in his humanity served everybody who had need of him.
>
> *Martin Luther* [5]

After I came to know the Lord in mid-life, He steered me into a job in the offshore oil industry that was a huge challenge, as there never seemed to be enough time and resources to do the work where I could say I was working unto the Lord. But amid these daily difficulties He showed me two things. First, was the importance of faith in maintaining that vital presence of the Holy Spirit in my life so that what I was unable to do in my own strength at work, He was able to accomplish through His divine providence. Second, was that He had placed me in this company for His purposes so that I could be a witness for Him by allowing His presence to be demonstrated in my life through love towards my coworkers.

These two pillars of Christianity as spoken of by Jesus in the Greatest Commandment are both a constant challenge and great reward. To keep them in the forefront of my busy days I wrote this simple prose and placed it in a visible location on my office desk.

A LIFE OF FAITH AND LOVE

A life of faith
comes from a day of faith,
comes from an hour of faith,
comes from a moment of faith.
Teach me, O Lord, to live each moment in faith.

A life of love
comes from a day of love,
comes from an hour of love,
comes from a moment of love.
Teach me, O Lord, to live each moment with love.

Teach me, O Lord, to live each moment in faith with love.

Reflection and Discussion

In what ways has God given you influence or authority over others—in your family, in your work life, in your church and social activities—and do you use this influence or authority to serve others or to serve yourself?

Challenge for This Week

God wants us to be transmitters of the love that He pours into us by acting in love towards others. As you read the Bible verses this week ask God in prayer to increase your love for Him and to increase your desire to act with love towards others.

Memory Verse

Your attitude should be the same as that of Christ Jesus... taking the very nature of a servant (Philippians 2:5, 7b).

Daily Bible Readings for Week 6

Day 1, read Matthew 20:20-28

Key verse: *"Instead, whoever wants to become great among you must be your servant... just as the Son of Man did not come to be served, but to serve..."* (vv. 26b, 28a).

Day 2, read Luke 22:24-27

Key verse: *"Instead, the greatest among you should be like the youngest, and the one who rules like the one who serves"* (v. 26b).

Day 3, read John 13:1-17

Key verse: *"I have set you an example that you should do as I have done for you"* (v. 15).

Day 4, read Galatians 5:1-15

Key verse: *You, my brothers, were called to be free. But do not use your freedom to indulge the sinful nature; rather, serve one another in love* (v. 13).

Day5, read Philippians 2:1-11

Key verse: *Your attitude should be the same as that of Christ Jesus: ... taking the very* nature *of a servant...* (vv. 5, 7b).

Day 6, read 1 Peter 4:7-11

Key verse: *Each one should use whatever gift he has received to serve others, faithfully administering God's grace in its various forms* (v. 10).

Week 6 Journal

Make notes about your journey with Jesus this week; for example, how He led you; how He spoke to you (see *Your Voice* on pages 4); how God worked providentially in your circumstances; breakthroughs and setbacks.

Note: there is additional journal space at the end of the guidebook.

Week 7: Worry

May I remember that it is not for me to worry about tomorrow, but to gladly do Your will this day.

Christ said: "*So do not worry, saying, 'What shall we eat?' or 'What shall we drink?' or 'What shall we wear?' For the [unbelievers] run after all these things, and your heavenly Father knows that you need them. But seek first his kingdom and his righteousness, and all these things will be given to you as well*" (Matthew 6:31-33).

These words of Jesus tell us that we remove worry not by our own strength, but by seeking God's kingdom and His righteousness.

> With regard to the problem that is pressing in on you right now, are you "*fixing your eyes on Jesus*" (Hebrews 12:2) and receiving peace from Him? If so, He will be a gracious blessing of peace exhibited in and through you. But if you try to worry your way out of the problem, you destroy His effectiveness in you…. When a person confers with Jesus Christ, the confusion stops, because there is no confusion in Him.
>
> Oswald Chambers [6]

From my first recollections as a child I always wanted to do things well, to be in control of situations so that no unexpected circumstances would upset my plans, and most of all to do things my way. These characteristics can be most beneficial in our society and often lead to success in this world, but the flip side is a propensity to worry.

Since coming to know the Lord, I have often wished that He would just switch off my old way of thinking and switch on a full measure of His presence, but that is not how the Lord works. He wants us to yield to Him by our own choices and draw daily closer to Him and in so doing lose our fears and worries.

In this process, which can be long and painful, we need to continuously recognize how great, mighty and awesome our Lord is, and I penned these simple phrases to remind me of this truth.

WHY SO FEARFUL?

Why so fearful, oh, my heart?
The Lord is my comfort and my confidence:
the great and mighty God!

Why so fearful, oh, my soul?
The Lord is my rock and my refuge:
the great and awesome God!

Why so fearful, oh, my mind?
The Lord is my shield and my strength:
the great, mighty and awesome God!

Reflection and Discussion

What situations make you worry at home, at work, in all of life?

Do these worries spill over into other parts of your life and affect your relationship with other people and your witness for Jesus Christ?

Challenge for This Week

As you read the passages of scripture this week, also pray that the Lord will show you how to build your faith in Him so that the things you worry about diminish.

Memory Verse

Cast all your anxiety on him because he cares for you (1 Peter 5:7).

Daily Bible Readings for Week 7

Day 1, read Psalm 55:1-8, 16-19 and 22-23

Key verse: *Cast your cares on the LORD and he will sustain you; he will never let the righteous fall* (v. 22).

Day 2, read Psalm 143:1-12

Key verse: *Teach me to do your will, for you are my God; may your good Spirit lead me on level ground* (v. 10).

Day 3, read Matthew 6:25-34

Key verse: *"Therefore do not worry about tomorrow, for tomorrow will worry about itself. Each day has enough trouble of its own"* (v. 34).

Day 4, read Mark 4:1-8 and 13-20

Key verse: *"Still others, like seed sown among thorns, hear the word; but the worries of this life... come in and choke the word, making it unfruitful"* (vv. 18, 19).

Day 5, read Luke 21:5-36

Key verse: *"Be careful, or your hearts will be weighed down with... the anxieties of life, and that day will close on you unexpectedly like a trap"* (v. 34).

Day 6, read 1 Peter 5:6-11

Key verse: *Cast all your anxiety on him because he cares for you* (v. 7).

Week 7 Journal

Make notes about your journey with Jesus this week; for example, how He led you; how He spoke to you (see *Your Voice* on page 4); how God worked providentially in your circumstances; breakthroughs and setbacks.

Note: there is additional journal space at the end of the guidebook.

Week 8: Peace

May I know the peace and confidence that comes from following Your way.

The Lord tells us in Isaiah 32:17, "*The fruit of righteousness will be peace; the effect of righteousness will be quietness and confidence forever.*" Consequently, to find this peace of mind and confidence the Lord promises, we must find righteousness—we must be "right" with the Lord.

> When man was created he was at peace with God, with himself, and with his fellow humans. But when he rebelled against God, his fellowship with God was broken. He was no longer at peace with himself. And he was no longer at peace with others.
>
> Can these dimensions of peace ever be restored? The Bible says yes. It tells us man alone cannot do what is necessary to heal the brokenness in his relationships—but God can, and has.
>
> *Billy Graham* [7]

I had made a bad decision in selling a car that resulted in the title of the vehicle remaining in my name even as I had lost contact with the person I had sold it to. Subsequently, he became involved in a hit-and-run accident and committed multiple parking offenses. This was a time of great stress for my wife and me as we faced the challenges of the police investigation, insurance claims, parking fines, and trying to resolve the problem with the local Department of Motor Vehicles. But as hard as we tried to resolve the issue, nothing happened, and we remained liable for all the offenses.

The height of the crisis corresponded with the time we had made arrangements to take a one-week vacation to Yellowstone National Park; therefore, we seriously considered cancelling our vacation to spend our time searching for the car I had sold, and the person who was creating this mayhem for us. The Lord placed on our hearts to proceed with the vacation, however, and in doing so we found His peace.

When we returned from the vacation the stress also inevitably returned, but a still small voice in my mind said, "Go back to the DMV". There, we quickly found out that the records had been changed so that the title was now in the name of "persons unknown". God's grace had worked in an amazing, providential way to start us on the road to resolving all the problems. This inspired me to write this one-sentence poem that I often return to reconnect with my Lord and His peace and grace.

HIS PEACE
Know His peace,
know His pace,
by His Spirit,
by His grace.

Reflection and Discussion

In what situations do you have stress instead of peace, frustration instead of quietness, and feelings of inadequacy instead of confidence?

Have you been able to experience the peace of God that transcends all understanding at work?

Challenge for This Week

As you read the daily scriptures this week, also pray to Jesus for the faith to release all difficult situations to Him so that you would know the peace of God.

Memory Verse

The fruit of righteousness will be peace; the effect of righteousness will be quietness and confidence forever (Isaiah 32:17).

Daily Bible Readings for Week 8

Day 1, read Isaiah 9:2-7

Key verse: *For to us a child is born, to us a son is given, and the government will be on his shoulders. And he will be called Wonderful Counselor, Mighty God, Everlasting Father, Prince of Peace* (v. 6).

Day 2, read Jeremiah 17:5-8

Key verse: *"But blessed is the man who trusts in the LORD, whose confidence is in him"* (v. 7).

Day 3, read John 14:15-27

Key verse: *"Peace I leave with you; my peace I give you. I do not give to you as the world gives. Do not let your hearts be troubled and do not be afraid"* (v. 27).

Day 4, read Romans 5:1-11

Key verse: *Therefore, since we have been justified through faith, we have peace with God through our Lord Jesus Christ...* (v. 1).

Day 5, read Philippians 4:4-9

Key verse: *And the peace of God, which transcends all understanding, will guard your hearts and your minds in Christ Jesus* (v. 7).

Day 6, read Hebrews 12:1-13

Key verse: *No discipline seems pleasant at the time, but painful. Later on, however, it produces a harvest of righteousness and peace for those who have been trained by it* (v. 11).

Week 8 Journal

Make notes about your journey with Jesus this week; for example, how He led you; how He spoke to you (see *Your Voice* on page 4); how God worked providentially in your circumstances; breakthroughs and setbacks.

Note: there is additional journal space at the end of the guidebook.

Week 9: Joy

May I know the joy that springs from this peace as I see You move in the lives of those who love You.

Joy is one of the fruit of the Spirit that Paul mentions in his letter to the Galatians where he writes, "*But the fruit of the Spirit is love, joy, peace, patience, kindness, goodness, faithfulness, gentleness and self-control*" (Galatians 5:22-23). These then are the benefits that come to us, and can shine through us as a witness to others, when we follow the Lord's way.

> Why do I not rejoice much more over my holy and faithful Savior, Christ, who gave himself for me and to me wholly as my own? Shame on me because of my unbelief, that my heart is not here full of laughter and eternal joy, when I hear and know how he says to me through his Word that he will be my beloved bridegroom.
>
> *Martin Luther [8]*

It was a difficult trip from the beginning. The flight out of Houston to Abu Dhabi via New York was cancelled because of snow in New York. After a lengthy delay and rerouting I arrived at my destination only to find that my bags were still in Amsterdam. When I checked into the hotel they put me in a room that was above the main disco bar with music blasting in my ears to 2:00 a.m. in the morning. The next day I arrived at our site office to find the internet connection had slowed to a crawl, and the relations with our client were at a desperately low level.

In these difficult days, I continued in my commitment to daily Bible reading and prayer, and the Lord "guided" me to passages relating to praise and joy. Through this continued fellowship with our Lord, I learned the wonderful lesson that our joy does not depend on our circumstances; rather, our joy depends solely on maintaining our fellowship with Him so that we do not quench the Holy Spirit.

THE JOY OF BUSINESS TRAVEL

Have joy when your flight gets delayed.
Have joy when your bags get mislaid.

Have joy when your hotel room is too noisy to sleep.
Have joy in situations that make you want to weep.

Have joy when your internet connection fails.
Have joy when your major client bails.

Have joy because God knows all these things.
Have joy because He will lift you on His wings.

Reflection and Discussion

Make an assessment of the extent to which the fruit of the Spirit are present in your life: always (4), most of the time (3), sometimes (2), infrequently (1), never (0).

Love ( )	Joy ( )	Peace ( )
Patience ( )	Kindness ( )	Goodness ( )
Faithfulness ( )	Gentleness ( )	Self-control ( )

Are these fruit of the Spirit more or less evident when you are at work?

Challenge for This Week

In prayer ask Jesus to open your heart to understand what is keeping you from experiencing the full blessings of the Holy Spirit and what actions you need to take to remove these barriers.

Memory Verse

"I have told you this so that my joy may be in you and that your joy may be complete" (John 15:11).

Daily Bible Readings for Week 9

Day 1, read Nehemiah 8:1-18

Key verse: *Nehemiah said, "Go and enjoy choice food and sweet drinks and send some to those who have nothing prepared. This day is sacred to our Lord. Do not grieve, for the joy of the* Lord *is your strength"* (v. 10).

Day 2, read Psalm 95:1-11

Key verse: *Come, let us sing for joy to the LORD; let us shout aloud to the Rock of our salvation* (v. 1).

Day 3, read Psalm 100:1-5

Key verse: *Worship the LORD with gladness; come before Him with joyful songs* (v. 2).

Day 4, read Isaiah 55:8-13

Key verse: *You will go out in joy and be led forth in peace; the mountains and hills will burst into song before you, and all the trees of the field will clap their hands* (v. 12).

Day 5, read John 15:1-17

Key verse: *"I have told you this so that my joy may be in you and that your joy may be complete"* (v. 11).

Day 6, read James 1:2-8

Key verse: *Consider it pure joy, my brothers, whenever you face trials of many kinds...* (v. 2).

Week 9 Journal

Make notes about your journey with Jesus this week; for example, how He led you; how He spoke to you (see *Your Voice* on page 4); how God worked providentially in your circumstances; breakthroughs and setbacks.

Note: there is additional journal space at the end of the guidebook.

Week 10: Prayer

May I know that all of this is possible as I pray and give praise in all things.

How is it possible to live in the Lord's way in a world where the prevailing values contradict the values of our Lord in almost every instance?

By our own strength it is not possible. Only when we commit our lives to the Lord—communicating with Him daily through the Bible and through prayer—can His truth be manifested in our lives. As Paul said, *"Be joyful always; pray continually; give thanks in all circumstances, for this is God's will for you in Christ Jesus"* (1 Thessalonians 5:16-18).

> When a general chooses the place from which he intends to strike the enemy, he pays the most attention to those points he thinks most important in the fight. On the battlefield of Waterloo there was a farmhouse which Wellington immediately saw as the key to the situation. He did not spare his troops in his endeavor to hold that point: the victory depended on it. So it actually happened. It is the same in the conflict between the believer and the powers of darkness. The place of private prayer is the key, the strategic position where decisive victory is obtained.
>
> *Andrew Murray* [9]

Just as our interaction with a dear friend can take on many forms, so our interaction in prayer with our Dearest Friend should take on many forms. Take time to read the writing below together with the referenced Bible verses and the Holy Spirit will open new vistas to an expanded and enriched time of prayer with our Lord.

THE BEAUTIFUL GIFT OF PRAYER

Thank you, Father, for the beautiful gift of prayer.

Thank You for prayer in solitude (see Matthew 6:6).

Thank You for prayer with other believers (see Acts 1:14).

Thank You for prayer in the details of life (see Philippians 4:6).

Thank You for prayer in the important decisions of life (see Luke 6:12-13).

Thank You for prayer at the start of the day (see Mark 1:35.).

Thank You for prayer at the end of the day (see Matthew 14:23).

Thank You for prayer with joy (see Philippians 1:3-5).

Thank You for prayer with anguish (see Mark 14:34-36).

Thank You for prayer with certainty (see Mark 11:24).

Thank You for prayer with doubt (see Romans 8:26).

Thank You for prayer by many (see 2 Corinthians 1:10b-11).

Thank You for prayer by few (see James 5:16b).

Thank You for prayer with fellowship (see Acts 2:42).

Thank You for prayer with fasting (see Acts 14:23).

Thank You for prayer in all things (see 1 Thessalonians 5:16-18).

Thank you, Father, for this beautiful gift of prayer.

Reflection and Discussion

If you have been meeting daily with our Lord in His Word and in prayer for the last ten weeks you will have seen God blessing your life in various ways. Identify some of these blessings.

If you have been unable to meet daily with our Lord identify the barriers that prevent you from doing this.

Challenge for This Week

The beginning and the end of making the changes in our lives—to resolve our fears and to be a true witness for Him—is a closer walk with Jesus. Think and pray about any barriers in your life that need to be removed to have this closer walk with our Savior.

Memory Verse

Be joyful always; pray continually; give thanks in all circumstances, for this is God's will for you in Christ Jesus (1 Thessalonians 5:16-18).

Daily Bible Readings for Week 10

Day 1, read Psalm 17:1-15

Key verse: *I call on you, O God, for you will answer me; give ear to me and hear my prayer* (v. 6).

Day 2, read Matthew 6:5-15

Key verse: *"But when you pray, go into your room, close the door and pray to your Father, who is unseen. Then your Father, who sees what is done in secret, will reward you"* (v. 6).

Day 3, read Luke 18:1-14

Key verse: *Then Jesus told his disciples a parable to show them that they should always pray and not give up* (v. 1).

Day 4, read Luke 22:39-46

Key verse: *And being in anguish, he prayed more earnestly, and his sweat was like drops of blood falling to the ground* (v. 44).

Day 5, read Colossians 4:2-6

Key verse: *Devote yourselves to prayer, being watchful and thankful* (v. 2).

Day 6, read James 5:13-20

Key verse: *The prayer of a righteous man is powerful and effective* (v. 16b).

Week 10 Journal

Make notes about your journey with Jesus this week; for example, how He led you; how He spoke to you (see *Your Voice* on page 4); how God worked providentially in your circumstances; breakthroughs and setbacks.

Note: there is additional journal space at the end of the guidebook.

Part II: Abide in Him

Oh how difficult it is to abide in the Lord: difficult in times of great activity and difficult in times of low activity, difficult in times of forward progress and difficult in times of frustration, difficult in times of being honored and difficult in times of being criticized. But we must try.

To abide in Him is to recognize the deceit in our hearts.

To abide in Him is to recognize the love and power available by allowing the Spirit of Christ to flow into our hearts.

To abide in Him is to work diligently and responsibly for the Lord.

To abide in Him is to wait quietly on the Lord.

To abide in Him is to know that the pathway He blocks no one can clear.

To abide in Him is to know that the doors He opens no one can shut.

To abide in Him is to suffer through many trials and hardships.

To abide in Him is to know that the Lord will not let us be tempted beyond what we can endure.

And if we try, we find that His yoke is easy and His burden is light as all things do work together for those who love God.

Amen.

When we belong to the Lord and earnestly seek His way, He is not content for us only to follow a set of Christian principles; He wants us to abide in Him. Jesus makes this clear in John 15:4 where He says, *"Abide in Me, and I in you. As the branch cannot bear fruit of itself, unless it abides in the vine, so neither can you, unless you abide in Me"* (NASB).

Reminder

For this guidebook to help you have an intimate, living relationship with our Lord and Savior Jesus Christ, it is important to continue the discipline of meeting with Him <u>daily</u> in His Word and prayer.

Week 11: Our Deceitful Hearts

To abide in Him is to recognize the deceit in our hearts.

A painful step in learning to abide in Christ is to recognize we are deceitful by nature. We justify our worldly natures in a spirit of pride and defiance against the written Word of God and the nudging of our consciences. Christ leaves no doubt about this when He says, *"For from within, out of men's hearts, come evil thoughts, sexual immorality, theft, murder, adultery, greed, malice, deceit, lewdness, envy, slander, arrogance and folly"* (Mark 7:21-22).

> There is one vice of which no man in the world is free; which everyone in the world loathes when he sees it in someone else; and of which hardly any people, except Christians, even imagine they are guilty themselves....
>
> The vice I am talking about is Pride or Self-Conceit.... Unchastity, anger, greed, drunkenness, and all that, are mere fleabites in comparison: it was through Pride that the devil became the devil. Pride leads to every other vice: it is the complete anti-God state of mind.
>
> *C. S. Lewis* [10]

At the time I came to know the Lord and for two years thereafter we lived in Santa Barbara, California, and early each Saturday morning I would take our son for a long walk along a quiet beach on the west side of town. This beach had many rock pools and abundant life in the deeper waters that would yield a bumper crop of sea shells for most of our visits. Also I quickly realized that the largest and most difficult to find shells would be washed up onto the beach after a storm: the stronger the storm, the bigger the harvest of these beautiful shells.

Our walk with the Lord is like this, when, after a crisis or major problem in our lives, He provides us with some beautiful insight that draws us closer to Him. It was after one such crisis that the Lord revealed to me there was sin and deceit in my life, which was so much part of me, I desperately wanted to hold onto it. Therefore, I needed to ask Jesus to tear away this sin as I could not readily yield it to the urgings of His Spirit. The storm was not easy, but the revelation and release were gems to find and treasures to keep as captured in this prayer.

THAT I MAY LOVE YOU MORE

Dear Lord Jesus,
Show me who I am,
    that I may know You more,
    that I may love You more.

Take away my sins,
    that I may know You more,
    that I may love You more.

Tear away my sins,
    that I may know You more,
    that I may love You more.

Leave only Your Spirit,
    that I may know You more,
    that I may love You more.

That I may know You more,
    that I may love You more.
Amen.

Reflection and Discussion

Are there things in your life that you know are not right with God, but you have trouble releasing to Him?

Are there things that you enjoy receiving compliments about from other people at work, but in your heart you know they do not honor God?

Challenge for This Week

As you read the scriptures and pray this week, seek to surrender all things to Jesus Christ so that you may see the fullness of the deceit in your heart and release more of your worldly nature to His presence.

Memory Verse

The heart is deceitful above all things and beyond cure. Who can understand it? (Jeremiah 17:9).

Daily Bible Readings for Week 11

Day 1, read Genesis 6:1-8

Key verse: *The L*ORD *saw how great man's wickedness on the earth had become, and that every inclination of the thoughts of his heart was only evil all the time* (v. 5).

Day 2, read Genesis 8:15-22

Key verse: *The L*ORD *smelled the pleasing aroma and said in his heart: "Never again will I curse the ground because of man, even though every inclination of his heart is evil from childhood"* (v. 21a).

Day 3, read Jeremiah 17:5-10

Key verse: *The heart is deceitful above all things and beyond cure. Who can understand it?* (v. 9).

Day 4, read Mark 7:1-23

Key verse: *"For from within, out of men's hearts, come evil thoughts, sexual immorality, theft, murder, adultery, greed, malice, deceit, lewdness, envy, slander, arrogance and folly"* (vv. 21-22).

Day 5, read Galatians 5:16-21

Key verse: *For the sinful nature desires what is contrary to the Spirit, and the Spirit what is contrary to the sinful nature* (v. 17a).

Day 6, read Colossians 3:1-11

Key verse: *Put to death, therefore, whatever belongs to your earthly nature: sexual immorality, impurity, lust, evil desires and greed, which is idolatry* (v. 5).

Week 11 Journal

Make notes about your journey with Jesus this week; for example, how He led you; how He spoke to you (see *Your Voice* on page 4); how God worked providentially in your circumstances; breakthroughs and setbacks.

Note: there is additional journal space at the end of the guidebook.

Week 12: Christ's Love and Power

To abide in Him is to recognize the love and power available by allowing the Spirit of Christ to flow into our hearts.

Once we acknowledge and repent of our sinful natures, the Lord does not leave us without recourse. On the contrary, He promises and provides us with much greater strength, both in love toward our fellow men and in power to carry out our responsibilities. Paul describes this in his letter to Timothy where he writes, *"For God did not give us a spirit of timidity, but a spirit of power, of love and of self-discipline"* (2 Timothy 1:7).

> Jesus instructs us to pray, "Your kingdom come." By this prayer we are taking our role as members of a race who once betrayed the King and forfeited His intended purposes into the claws of the adversary. But now, as His redeemed sons and daughters, He has endowed us with restored "kingdom authority," through prayer to welcome His entry into every need and pain of this planet.
>
> The power is God's, but the privilege and responsibility to pray are ours. So, let us hear and understand Jesus' words and come together at His throne, expecting and receiving the flow of the Holy Spirit's power.
>
> *Jack W. Hayford* [11]

Eighteen to twenty miles into a marathon the runners often "hit the wall" when they deplete their bodies of glycogen, the main source of energy for strenuous exercise, and they quickly experience serious fatigue. This phase of the race really test the runners' endurance as they must start burning stored fat, which does not burn so readily as the glycogen, and the temptation to drop out of the race can be overwhelming.

I experienced this phenomenon of "hitting the wall" in my walk with the Lord. After I had followed my Savior as faithfully as I could for nineteen years, I suddenly felt that I could not go on and my steps became slow and labored. In this struggle, the Lord whispered to my spirit that my energy may be depleted, but His tank of energy was always full and available to all who believed. Soon I was able to say to my Lord, "Lead me on!"

LEAD ME ON

Lead me on, Lord Jesus, lead me on!
Make my feet like the feet of a deer, to enable
me to go on the heights. Broaden the path
beneath me so that my ankles do not turn.

Lead me on, Lord Jesus, lead me on!
Renew my strength so that I can soar on wings
like an eagle, so that I can run and not grow
weary, walk and not be faint.

Lead me on, Lord Jesus, lead me on!
Help me strain toward what is ahead; to press
on toward the goal to win the prize for which
You have called me heavenward.

Lead me on, Lord Jesus, lead me on!

Reflection and Discussion

When have you felt the Spirit of God powerfully intervene in your life at work?

Have you experienced the power, love, and self-discipline that Paul writes to Timothy about in 2 Timothy 1:7?

Challenge for This Week

Ask God that you may not only overcome your weaknesses, but that you may also be filled with His power to live as He would have you live.

Memory Verse

For God did not give us a spirit of timidity, but a spirit of power, of love and of self-discipline (2 Timothy 1:7).

Daily Bible Readings for Week 12

Day 1, read Luke 24:36-49

Key verse: *"I am going to send you what my Father has promised; but stay in the city until you have been clothed with power from on high"* (v. 49).

Day 2, read Acts 1:1-11

Key verse: *"But you will receive power when the Holy Spirit comes on you; and you will be my witnesses… to the ends of the earth"* (v. 8).

Day 3, read 2 Corinthians 13:1-10

Key verse: *For to be sure, he was crucified in weakness, yet he lives by God's power. Likewise, we are weak in him, yet by God's power we will live with him to serve you* (v. 4).

Day 4, read Ephesians 3:7-21

Key verse: *I pray that out of his glorious riches he may strengthen you with power through his Spirit in your inner being…* (v. 16).

Day 5, read 1 Thessalonians 1:2-10

Key verse: *… because our gospel came to you not simply with words, but also with power, with the Holy Spirit and with deep conviction* (v. 5a).

Day 6, read 2 Peter 1:3-11

Key verse: *His divine power has given us everything we need for life and godliness through our knowledge of him who called us by his own glory and goodness* (v. 3).

Week 12 Journal

Make notes about your journey with Jesus this week; for example, how He led you; how He spoke to you (see *Your Voice* on pages 4); how God worked providentially in your circumstances; breakthroughs and setbacks.

Note: there is additional journal space at the end of the guidebook.

Week 13: Work

To abide in Him is to work diligently and responsibly for the Lord.

Although following Jesus at work is the primary focus of all this book, this chapter brings out some additional specific Biblical perspectives.

Work has been a vital part of man's relationship with God ever since He created Adam and Eve. Consequently, our work, regardless of its nature—paid or unpaid, vocation or obligation—is an expression of God's will for us.

Nevertheless, God has given us a free choice: to work as working for Him or to work as working for ourselves. And Paul makes it clear which choice we should make: "*Whatever you do, work at it with all your heart, as working for the Lord, not for men, since you know that you will receive an inheritance from the Lord as a reward. It is the Lord Christ you are serving*" (Colossians 3:23-24).

> God uses everything in the workplace to train our character. He uses the evil we face, the people we can't stand, the circumstances of tension and pressure, the tedium of long afternoons, the solicitations to compromise, the irritations of angry customers, the interruptions, the financial reversals, the deals that fall through, even the traffic on the way home—He uses all of it to make us like Jesus.
>
> *Doug Sherman and William Hendricks* [12]

I had worked in the oil industry for over fifteen years and it concerned me that so many people were not excited and motivated in their work life. Eventually, I wrote a book on this topic, which was soundly rejected by publishers and literary agents alike, but the yearning remained. This led me to leave my job to focus on this passion. My own writing skills soon dried up, however, and in desperation I turned to the Lord. I then remained in "the school of my Lord" for two years soaking up knowledge of Him and writing about Him, but when this period came to an end—instead of granting my heart's desire to become a published author and public speaker—He sent me back into the workplace and soon showed me that here was one of His main harvest fields.

It took me a long time to gain a good understanding of how to live for Christ in the secular workplace, but I eventually learned that each trial and frustration had kingdom opportunities to witness of His presence and His love.

THE BLESSINGS OF WORK

Think of work as a blessed task...
because through the trials of work we are
drawn closer to God.

Think of work as a vibrant opportunity...
because by our attitude to work we can
spread the fragrance of the knowledge of
Jesus to those who are lost.

Think of work as having eternal significance...
because we can shine like stars in the
universe at work as we hold out the word of
life to those who need Jesus.

Reflection and Discussion

Think of the times when you are able to work "as working for the Lord." How does this differ from the times when you struggle?

Reread *The Blessings of Work*, above, and think about how each of the verses apply to your work life.

Challenge for This Week

In prayer continue to seek a closer walk with Jesus and the presence of His Spirit so that you may have the desire, patience and perseverance to always see your work as serving Him.

Memory Verse

Whatever you do, work at it with all your heart, as working for the Lord, not for men, since you know that you will receive an inheritance from the Lord as a reward. It is the Lord Christ you are serving (Colossians 3:23-24).

Daily Bible Readings for Week 13

Day 1, read Genesis 2:4-17

Key verse: *The Lord God took the man and put him in the Garden of Eden to work it and take care of it* (v. 15).

Day 2 read Genesis 3:17-24

Key verse: *To Adam he said... "Cursed is the ground because of you; through painful toil you will eat of it all the days of your life"* (v. 17).

Day 3, read Ecclesiastes 2:17-26

Key verse: *A man can do nothing better than to eat and drink and find satisfaction in his work. This too, I see, is from the hand of God, for without him, who can eat or find enjoyment?* (vv. 24-25).

Day 4, read Matthew 25:14-30

Key verse: *"His master replied, 'Well done, good and faithful servant! You have been faithful with a few things; I will put you in charge of many things'"* (v. 21).

Day 5, read John 6:25-40

Key verse: *"Do not work for food that spoils, but for food that endures to eternal life, which the Son of Man will give you"* (v. 27a).

Day 6, read Ephesians 6:5-8

Key verse: *Serve wholeheartedly, as if you were serving the Lord, not men...* (v. 7).

Week 13 Journal

Make notes about your journey with Jesus this week; for example, how He led you; how He spoke to you (see *Your Voice* on page 4); how God worked providentially in your circumstances; breakthroughs and setbacks.

Note: there is additional journal space at the end of the guidebook.

Week 14: Waiting

To abide in Him is to wait quietly on the Lord.

One of the hardest things to do is to wait quietly on the Lord, especially when we seem to stagnate as others succeed and pass us by. But in Psalm 37:7 David speaks clearly to us and gives us hope, *"Be still before the LORD and wait patiently for him; do not fret when men succeed in their ways...."*

> It is hard to be called by God and live in our society at the same time. In America, when the action impulse comes, action follows immediately. No patience required—technology and culture let us proceed immediately. Not so with God. Immediately when He calls us, He postpones our sending. There is other work to be done first.
>
> *Patrick M. Morley* [12]

Exodus 40:36-38 tells us, *"In all the travels of the Israelites, whenever the cloud lifted from above the tabernacle, they would set out; but if the cloud did not lift, they did not set out—until the day it lifted. So the cloud of the LORD was over the tabernacle by day, and fire was in the cloud by night, in the sight of all the house of Israel during all their travels."*

Oh how frustrating it must have been for the Israelites not to move at their own pace to the Promised Land. I can imagine a beautiful clear day in the Sinai Peninsula that was ideal for travelling, but the pillar of cloud didn't budge. Maybe that one day turned into a week or even a month, and still the cloud showed no signs of movement—how they must have murmured against the Lord, but to no avail.

I confess that I have frequently been like the Israelites, thinking I know much better than my Lord which path I should take, the times when I should be moving forward, and the times when I should be holding back. Nevertheless, the cloud of His Presence, now the Holy Spirit living in me, has never been moved by my meager agenda, but only by His perfect agenda for my life.

BE STILL

I sought to do God's will, and God said, "Be still."

I tried to accomplish the plans I had laid out, but God said, "Be still."

I sought all manner of ways and all types of advice to achieve my goals, but God said, "Be still."

I pined over the glory of past accomplishments; I paced the room like a caged animal; I cried out to the Lord, "This cannot be your will!" But the Lord said, "Be still."

Reflection and Discussion

Where do you see that you have lost ground to others (or may lose ground) by waiting for the Lord at work?

What is the hardest part for you about waiting on the Lord?

Challenge for This Week

Much prayer and support from fellow believers is needed to take us through one of the hardest parts of our growth in the Lord—waiting for Him. Always be diligent in prayer, faithful in reading His Word, and unashamed in seeking support from fellow believers.

Memory Verse

Wait for the LORD; be strong and take heart and wait for the LORD (Psalm 27:14).

Daily Bible Readings for Week 14

Day 1, read Psalm 27:1-14

Key verse: *Wait for the LORD; be strong and take heart and wait for the LORD* (v. 14).

Day 2, read Psalm 37:1-40

Key verse: *Be still before the LORD and wait patiently for him; do not fret when men succeed in their ways, when they carry out their wicked schemes* (v. 7).

Day 3, read Psalm 46:1-11

Key verse: *"Be still, and know that I am God..."* (v. 10a).

Day 4, read Psalm 130:1-6

Key verse: *I wait for the* LORD, *my soul waits, and in his word I put my hope* (v. 5).

Day 5, read Hebrews 6:13-20

Key verse: *And so after waiting patiently, Abraham received what was promised* (v. 15).

Day 6, read 2 Peter 3:1-13

Key verse: *The Lord is not slow in keeping his promises, as some understand slowness. He is patient with you, not wanting anyone to perish, but everyone to come to repentance* (v.9).

Week 14 Journal

Make notes about your journey with Jesus this week; for example, how He led you; how He spoke to you (see *Your Voice* on page 4); how God worked providentially in your circumstances; breakthroughs and setbacks.

Note: there is additional journal space at the end of the guidebook.

Week 15: Open and Closed Doors

To abide in Him is to know that the pathway He blocks no one can clear.
To abide in Him is to know that the doors He opens no one can shut.

When we first follow our Savior, we often try to impose our own will as God's will, and this causes us to try to go along paths that the Lord does not intend for us to take. If we are faithful, however, the Lord will soon teach us the lessons of Revelation 3:7, *"What he opens no one can shut, and what he shuts no one can open."*

> He waits for us to despair of human strength and then intervenes with heavenly. God waits for us to give up and then—surprise!
>
> Has it been a while since you let God surprise you? It's easy to reach a point where [we believe] we have God figured out.
>
> We know exactly what God does. We break the code....
>
> Have you got God figured out? Have you got God captured on a flowchart...? If so, then listen. Listen to God's surprises.
>
> *Max Lucado* [14]

When the company I worked for moved from California to Houston I had an opportunity to move with them, but I was convinced that the Lord wanted my wife and me to stay in California, as many family members lived close by and I had an emerging leadership position in the prayer ministry at a large church. No matter how hard I tried, however, no doors opened for me to be able to earn a living.

After a ten-month search that more than depleted the severance package from the company move, I reluctantly, very reluctantly, called my previous employer in Houston to see if a move to rejoin them was still possible. Quickly doors opened: within six weeks we were living in Houston, I was restored to my previous management position, paid a bonus to move from California as if I had taken the original transfer offer, and my company benefits were restored based on my original start date with the company. So, in effect, I had received a tremendous blessing of having an eight-month paid sabbatical from the severance pay when the company moved, to then rejoin the company without penalty. Moreover, the blessings of living in Houston soon became clear to my wife and me and we marveled at the awesome grace of God. He knew which door to keep closed and which door to open. We only needed to open our eyes to His will.

OPEN OUR EYES, LORD

Open our eyes, Lord,
to see as You see.

Open our ears, Lord,
to hear what You say.

Open our mouths, Lord,
to speak of Your way.

Reflection and Discussion

Has a pathway that seemed so clear and right to you been blocked so that, try as you might, it has been impossible to go forward?

Has a door of opportunity unexpectedly and wonderfully opened up for you at work where there was no doubt in your mind that this was by the hand of God?

What has the Lord shown you in these situations or, if you have not experienced the Lord's leading in this way, why do you think that is?

Challenge for This Week

God opened and closed doors for Jonah in a most dramatic way (see days one to four of this week's Bible readings). When you read these passages, ask God to open your eyes to see if you are trying to impose your will rather than recognizing His sovereignty.

Memory Verse

What he opens no one can shut, and what he shuts no one can open (Revelation 3:7b).

Daily Bible Readings for Week 15

Day 1, read Jonah 1:1-17

Key verse: *But Jonah ran away from the Lord and... sailed for Tarshish to flee from the Lord* (v. 3).

Day 2, read Jonah 2:1-10

Key verse: *"In my distress I called to the Lord, and he answered me"* (v. 2a).

Day 3, read Jonah 3:1-10

Key verse: *Jonah obeyed the word of the Lord and went to Nineveh* (v. 3a).

Day 4, read Jonah 4:1-11

Key verse: *But Jonah was greatly displeased and became angry [at God]* (v. 1).

Day 5, read Matthew 7:7-12

Key verse: *"Ask and it will be given to you; seek and you will find; knock and the door will be opened to you"* (v. 7).

Day 6, read Revelation 3:7-13

Key verse: *"I know your deeds. See, I have placed before you an open door that no one can shut"* (v. 8a).

Week 15 Journal

Make notes about your journey with Jesus this week; for example, how He led you; how He spoke to you (see *Your Voice* on page 4); how God worked providentially in your circumstances; breakthroughs and setbacks.

Note: there is additional journal space at the end of the guidebook.

Week 16: Suffering

To abide in Him is to suffer through many trials and hardships.

Our old nature has such a strong hold on us, and we are so comfortable with it, that we cannot abide in Him unless we are driven helpless into Christ's arms. Paul expressed this as he wrote, "*We were under great pressure, far beyond our ability to endure.... But this happened that we might not rely on ourselves but on God...*" (2 Corinthians 1:8-9).

> Biblical teaching and personal experience thus combine to teach that suffering is the path to holiness or maturity. There is always an indefinable something about people who have suffered. They have a fragrance which others lack. They exhibit the meekness and gentleness of Christ.
>
> *John R. W. Stott* [15]

When we think of suffering the first thoughts are typically: chronic illness, loss of someone who is near and dear, a soldier in the front lines of battle, starving children in a third-world country. But there is also another kind of suffering that can be just as severe: suffering from the spiritual battle in the mind. The world and our own perspective of living in the world—that is to say, our unredeemed or sinful nature— are so real and immediate that to allow them to be changed by abiding in Jesus and knowing the living presence of the Holy Spirit results in intense spiritual battles. At times, it even seems that the Lord has abandoned us.

CROSSING THE DESERT

O Lord, why are You so far off? I am like a wanderer in the desert knowing only a mirage of Your Spirit.

O Lord, come soon, so that I may reach the refreshing oasis of Your touch.

May I not be put to shame; may others not be able to say, "He searched in vain to follow the Lord."

But if we are faithful, and at times it may seem that our faith is so weak that we are barely holding onto our Lord by our fingernails, we see that He never abandons us. Thus we take another step closer to a full life in Christ as a result of this suffering.

Reflections and Questions

True Christianity is not a broad and easy path, and by now you may have experienced situations in your walk with Jesus that have truly challenged your faith at home, at work and in all of life. Identify these situations.

Also, suffering through trials and hardships can, if we are faithful, produce a harvest of righteousness in drawing closer to Jesus Christ. Think about some of these blessings of your walk with our Savior.

Challenge for This Week

Always stay close to our Savior in prayer and in reading His Word, even if you do not sense the Lord's presence. Remember, God calls us to be faithful as an act of will, if necessary, overcoming our emotions by our choices.

Memory Verse

But rejoice that you participate in the sufferings of Christ, so that you may be overjoyed when his glory is revealed (1 Peter 4:13).

Daily Bible Readings for Week 16

Day 1, read Psalm 119:49-80

Key verse: *My comfort in my suffering is this: Your promise preserves my life* (v. 50).

Day 2, read Matthew 7:13-14 and 24-29

Key verse: *"But small is the gate and narrow the road that leads to life, and only a few find it"* (v. 14).

Day 3, read 2 Corinthians 1:3-11

Key verse: *For just as the sufferings of Christ flow over into our lives, so also through Christ our comfort overflows* (v. 5).

Day 4, read Philippians 3:1-11

Key verse: *What is more, I consider everything a loss compared to the surpassing greatness of knowing Christ Jesus my Lord, for whose sake I have lost all things. I consider them rubbish, that I may gain Christ...* (v. 8).

Day 5, read 1 Peter 1:3-12

Key verse: *These [trials] have come so that your faith... may be proved genuine and may result in praise, glory and honor when Jesus Christ is revealed* (v. 7).

Day 6, read 1 Peter 4:12-19

Key verse: *But rejoice that you participate in the sufferings of Christ, so that you may be overjoyed when his glory is revealed* (v. 13).

Week 16 Journal

Make notes about your journey with Jesus this week; for example, how He led you; how He spoke to you (see *Your Voice* on pages 4); how God worked providentially in your circumstances; breakthroughs and setbacks.

Note: there is additional journal space at the end of the guidebook.

Week 17: Temptation

To abide in Him is to know that the Lord will not let us be tempted beyond what we can endure.

Often the way is so hard that it seems it could not be God's will for us to suffer so much, or it seems that we do not have the faith to go on. Remember, however, *"No temptation has seized you except what is common to man. And God is faithful; he will not let you be tempted beyond what you can bear. But when you are tempted, he will also provide a way out so that you can stand up under it"* (1 Corinthians 10:13).

> Satan will most thoroughly and carefully examine us, and if he shall find us to be, like Achilles, vulnerable nowhere else but in our heel, he will shoot his arrows at our heel.
>
> I believe that Satan seldom attacks a man in a place of strength, but he generally looks for a weak point, the besetting sin. "There," says he, "there will I strike the blow." God help us in the hour of battle and the time of conflict! Indeed, unless the Lord should help us, this crafty foe might easily find enough joints in our armor and soon send the deadly arrow into our soul, so that we should fall down wounded before him.
>
> *Charles Spurgeon* [16]

A period of intense activity and responsibility occurred in my work life when I was about eight years into my walk with the Lord. I was the Quality Assurance Manager for a company that designed and built floating structures for the offshore oil industry. At the time, it was necessary for me to lead the company from a fairly unstructured way of doing business to certification to an international quality standard. The pressures of achieving this goal were intense and at times I would get up at 2:30 in the morning to go to work. During this period I tried to stay close to the Lord in daily Bible reading and prayer, but often it seemed that the Lord did not care about the difficulties I was facing and I wrote this prose.

MY COMPLAINT TO GOD

I wait for You, Lord,
  maybe not patiently, maybe not lovingly, but I wait.
I call on Your Name,
  but it seems as if You do not answer my calls, do not
  respond to my letters, do not give me an appointment.
I pray to You in despair,
  confess my sins as I know them, in private to You and
  to others who believe, and yet You remain silent.
Am I to say, "God is not there!"?
Am I to say, "I can wait no longer."?

No, I know You are there, Lord, and I know that You care,
  also I know that Your will will be done.
I will wait Lord, but remember Your servant for I am in
  anguish.

The temptation to turn away from the Lord was great and eventually I had to make a decision as to which was most important to me: to obtain the certification to the schedule set by the president of the company, or to be faithful to my Lord by not quenching His Spirit with the fruit of love, joy, peace, patience, kindness, goodness, faithfulness, gentleness and self-control (see Galatians 5:22-23). I chose my Lord and *He* brought the certification process to a successful conclusion.

Reflections and Questions

Have you been tempted to turn away from God because you felt He had abandoned you (or didn't seem relevant) in your work life?

Have you been tempted to turn away from God because of the enticements of the world and the flesh?

Challenge for This Week

As you face the trials and temptations of this week, pray earnestly to know in your heart, your soul, and your mind that not only has Jesus gone before us, but also He is always there with us, however difficult the circumstances of our lives may be.

Memory Verse

No temptation has seized you except what is common to man. And God is faithful; he will not let you be tempted beyond what you can bear. But when you are tempted, he will also provide a way out so that you can stand up under it (1 Corinthians 10:13).

Daily Bible Readings for Week 17

Day 1, read Psalm 34:1-22

Key verse: *A righteous man may have many troubles, but the L*ORD *delivers him from them all…* (v. 19).

Day 2, read Matthew 4:1-11

Key verse: *Jesus said to him, "Away from me, Satan! For it is written: 'Worship the Lord your God, and serve him only'"* (v. 10).

Day 3, read Ephesians 6:10-18

Key verse: *Therefore put on the full armor of God, so that when the day of evil comes, you may be able to stand your ground, and after you have done everything, to stand* (v. 13).

Day 4, read 1 Thessalonians 3:1-13

Key verse: *I was afraid that in some way the tempter might have tempted you and our efforts might have been useless* (v. 5b).

Day 5, read Hebrews 2:5-18

Key verse: *Because he himself suffered when he was tempted, he is able to help those who are being tempted* (v. 18).

Day 6, read James 1:12-18

Key verse: *When tempted, no one should say, "God is tempting me." For God cannot be tempted by evil, nor does he tempt anyone; but each one is tempted when, by his own evil desire, he is dragged away and enticed* (vv.13-14).

Week 17 Journal

Make notes about your journey with Jesus this week; for example, how He led you; how He spoke to you (see *Your Voice* on pages 4); how God worked providentially in your circumstances; breakthroughs and setbacks.

Note: there is additional journal space at the end of the guidebook.

Week 18: Things Work Together

And if we try, we find that His yoke is easy and His burden is light as all things do work together for those who love God.

What greater gift can we receive than to live with Christ in this life? *"Come to me, all you who are weary and burdened, and I will give you rest. Take my yoke upon you and learn from me, for I am gentle and humble in heart, and you will find rest for your souls. For my yoke is easy and my burden is light"* (Matthew 11:28-30). Then, as we continue to live with Him, we can know and experience that, *"God causes all things to work together for good to those who love God, to those who are called according to His purpose"* (Romans 8:28, NASB).

> It has always been the experience of the children of God that when we walk daily in the will of God, even that which looks like tragedy and loss in the end will turn out to be blessing and gain.
>
> *A. W. Tozer* [17]

The 2019 animated movie *Pilgrim's Progress,* which is based on John Bunyan's classic book, wonderfully depicts the trouble and challenges of the main character, Christian, as he seeks to follow Jesus.

Likewise, our walk with Jesus is filled with trouble and challenges that are often magnified, because Satan hates to see a person fully committed to their Savior. Consequently, we need to mature in faith so we can see how big our God is: far bigger than any trial we can possibly face, and far bigger than anything we can imagine. Then, as our eyes are opened to His majesty, we can worship Him in praise and thanksgiving regardless of our circumstances knowing He causes all things to work together for good to those who love Him.

YOU ARE TOO WONDERFUL

O Lord, You are too wonderful to me.
When I follow Your way:
You are the light in my eye;

> You are the glow on my face;
> You give me peace;
> You give me joy;
> You give me love;
> my spirit tastes the joy of being in Your
> eternal presence in heaven.
>
> O Lord, my heart's desire is to do Your will:
> to be the person You created me to be;
> to fulfill Your purpose for my life;
> to live in the house of the Lord forever.
>
> O Lord, You are too wonderful to me.

Reflections and Questions

Look beyond the storms of your daily life to see how Jesus is causing all things to work together for good at home, at work, and in all of life.

Identify these "things" as the Holy Spirit illuminates them to you.

Challenge for This Week

In prayer, give praise and thanks to Him who is carrying you through, even though there is still some way to go.

Memory Verse

And we know that in all things God works for the good of those who love him, who have been called according to his purpose (Romans 8:28).

Daily Bible Readings for Week 18

Day 1, read Exodus 33:12-23

Key verse: *The LORD replied, "My Presence will go with you, and I will give you rest"* (v. 14).

Day 2, read Psalm 16:1-11

Key verse: *You have made known to me the path of life; you will fill me with joy in your presence, with eternal pleasures at your right hand* (v. 11).

Day 3, read Psalm 84:1-12

Key verse: *Blessed are those whose strength is in you, who have set their hearts on pilgrimage* (v. 5).

Day 4, read Isaiah 40:25-31

Key verse: *... but those who hope in the* Lord *will renew their strength. They will soar on wings like eagles; they will run and not grow weary, they will walk and not be faint* (v. 31).

Day 5, read Habakkuk 3:17-19

Key verse: *The Sovereign* Lord *is my strength; he makes my feet like the feet of a deer, he enables me to go to the heights* (v. 19a).

Day 6, read Philippians 3:12-4:1

Key verse: *I press on toward the goal to win the prize for which God has called me heavenward in Christ Jesus* (v. 14).

Week 18 Journal

Make notes about your journey with Jesus this week; for example, how He led you; how He spoke to you (see *Your Voice* on pages 4); how God worked providentially in your circumstances; breakthroughs and setbacks.

Note: there is additional journal space at the end of the guidebook.

Part III: His Victory

Jesus Christ our Savior reigns. His is the victory!

His victory is when the nature of Jesus has uncontested ownership of our hearts.

His victory is when we live to fulfill the purpose Jesus has placed in our hearts.

His victory is when we follow the way of Jesus rather than the way of the world.

His victory is when we live daily in His presence with the fruit of the Spirit evident in our lives.

His victory is when we live daily in His presence with gifts of the Spirit bringing glory to God in our lives.

His victory is when we live daily in His presence with His abundant grace and power.

By this we are witnesses of His love.

Amen.

But thanks be to God! He gives us the victory through our Lord Jesus Christ (1 Corinthians 15:57).

We can know the fruit of the Spirit, our gifts of the Spirit, and participate in the Great Commission to *"go and make disciples"* (Matthew 28:19) when we ourselves are His disciples: when His nature has gained the victory over our old natures.

Reminder

For this guidebook to help you have an intimate, living relationship with our Lord and Savior Jesus Christ, it is important to continue the discipline of meeting with Him <u>daily</u> in His Word and prayer.

Week 19: Christ's Victory

Jesus Christ our Savior reigns. His is the victory!

As the Israelites left the desert to enter the Promised Land, so they entered a time of warfare that required complete reliance on God for victory. Also, as we leave the "desert of life" by choosing to allow Jesus to be Lord of our lives, we enter a time of warfare for our souls (mind, will, and emotions) where Satan wants to keep us captive to the ways of the world. *"But thanks be to God! He gives us the victory through our Lord Jesus Christ"* (1 Corinthians 15:57).

> Ultimately, as with Israel, the day dawns when there comes an end to the dismal old self-life of despair and discouragement. In an act of bold faith in God we decide to abandon ourselves and capitulate completely to Christ.... Then in implicit, unquestioning obedience we step out to comply with His wishes.
>
> This is a titanic pivot point in any person's walk with God. This is the crossing of the Jordan.... From then on there is no looking back. There is no returning to the weary old wilderness days of the wretched desert years.
>
> *W. Phillip Keller* [18]

Ephesians 6:11 tells us to *"put on the full armor of God so that you can take your stand against the devil's schemes."* This passage goes on to describe all the pieces of the armor of God which, with one exception, are defensive and protective. It is by this protection that we can stand the assaults of Satan, the prince of this world, as he works against us through life situations and people.

The one offensive weapon is "the sword of the Spirit, which is the Word of God." That is to say, the forces of evil are always turned back as we strike with the Word of God, and this confirms how essential it is for us to be in His Word so we can know and apply His Word in the days of battle.

THE LORD'S WARRIORS

Hallelujah, the Lord God Almighty reigns! His is the victory. We are His warriors.

In the clash of armies, the warrior must look to the Lord for guidance, for protection, for strength, for courage, for wisdom, for compassion, for rest, for healing, for recovery, for victory. So in our daily battles for the Lord, we must look to Him for these same things in our words and our deeds.

And as the battle rages, it is sometimes difficult to know if the Lord is there; sometimes it seems as if the forces that oppose us are too strong; sometimes it seems that those who are willing to fight for Him are too few; sometimes we wonder if it is worth going on.

But God is faithful. His victory is not by superior numbers. His protection is not by superior armor. His attack is not by superior weapons. The Lord's victory is His and His alone, made possible by His unfailing grace that can overcome all things.

Reflections and Questions

Identify some of the "battles" that you are experiencing at home, at work or in the rest of life.

Are any of these "battles" because you are withholding part of your life from our Lord Jesus and so quench the fullness of His Spirit?

Challenge for This Week

In prayerful submission to Jesus, ask Him to show you the true source of the struggles in your life and the true source of the power to overcome.

Memory Verse

He holds victory in store for the upright, he is a shield to those whose walk is blameless, for he guards the course of the just and protects the way of his faithful ones (Proverbs 2: 7-8).

Daily Readings for Week 19

Day 1, read Deuteronomy 20:1-4

Key verse: *"For the L*ORD *your God is the one who goes with you to fight for you… to give you victory"* (v. 4).

Day 2, read Psalm 44:1-8

Key verse: *I do not trust in my bow, my sword does not bring me victory; but you* give *us victory…* (vv. 6-7a).

Day 3, read Psalm 118:1-29

Key verse: *Shouts of joy and victory resound in the tents of the* righteous*: "The L*ORD*'s right hand has done mighty things!"* (v. 15).

Day 4, read Proverbs 2:1-8

Key verse: *He holds victory in store for the upright, he is a shield to those* whose *walk is blameless…* (v. 7).

Day 5, read Romans 8:28-39

Key verse: *No, in all these things we are more than conquerors through him who loved us* (v. 37).

Day 6, read 1 Corinthians 15:50-58

Key verse: *But thanks be to God! He gives us the victory through our Lord Jesus Christ* (v. 57).

Week 19 Journal

Make notes about your journey with Jesus this week; for example, how He led you; how He spoke to you (see *Your Voice* on page 4); how God worked providentially in your circumstances; breakthroughs and setbacks.

Note: there is additional journal space at the end of the guidebook.

Week 20: Only Jesus

*His victory is when the nature of Jesus has uncontested
ownership of our hearts.*

For Jesus to have uncontested ownership of our hearts, we have to get
to the point of recognizing our utter depravity apart from Him. It is
only then we can fully embrace the lordship of Jesus in our hearts.

> Victory begins with the name of Jesus on your lips; but it will
> not be consummated until the nature of Jesus is in your heart.
> This rule applies to every facet of spiritual warfare. Indeed,
> Satan will be allowed to come against the area of your
> weakness until you realize God's only answer is to become
> Christlike. As you begin to appropriate not just the name of
> Jesus, but His nature as well, the adversary will withdraw.
> Satan will not continue to assault you if the circumstances he
> designed to destroy you are now working to perfect you!
>
> *Francis Frangipane* [19]

The flight from Los Angeles to Boston required a change of planes in
Indianapolis, but the onward flight was cancelled and, after a four-
hour delay, I was rebooked on another flight that went via
Washington, causing an additional two hour delay. When I boarded
this flight my sense of communion with the Holy Spirit was lost, with
the fruit of the Spirit replaced by my own frustrations and I cried out
in silent prayer, "Oh Lord, how I fail You!"

Once the flight took off, however, I persevered to quiet my soul by
reading a book by Charles Spurgeon, but I had little enthusiasm for the
content and no release of my frustrations. Then the air hostess asked
to see the book and realizing from the title that I was a Christian she
went to get the book she was carrying with her, *The Three
Battlegrounds* by Francis Frangipane, which I quote from above.

What a blessing this book was as I understood for the first time
the nature of the spiritual battles in our minds. And, yes, it was also an

answer to those few words of prayer as I admitted my failings to the Lord. This understanding helped me on the road to releasing all to Jesus.

LORD MOST HIGH

Praise You, praise You, praise You, Lord Most High!
  You turn my pride into humility.
  You turn my deceit into purity.

Praise You, praise You, praise You, Lord Most High!
  You turn my self-seeking into loving.
  You turn my self-keeping into giving.

Praise You, praise You, praise You, Lord Most High!
  You turn my worry into peace.
  You turn my woe into joy.

Praise You, praise You, praise You, Lord Most High!
  You turn my caution into action.
  You turn my weakness into boldness.

Praise You, praise You, praise You, Lord Most High!

Reflections and Questions

The way to victory in Jesus inevitably includes situations when we fail Him. Identify those situations that have occurred in your life.

Have you allowed Jesus to restore you after these failures and experienced the blessings of His forgiveness?

Has your faith been strengthened so that you can avoid future failures?

Challenge for This Week

Get apart with the Lord and pour out your heart to him. Do not leave His presence until you have transacted this most important decision: "Yes, Lord, I surrender all to You."

Memory Verse

Whoever claims to live in him must walk as Jesus did (1 John 2:6).

Daily Readings for Week 20

Day 1, read Psalm 32:1-11

Key verse: *Then I acknowledged my sin to you and did not cover up my iniquity. I said, "I will confess my transgressions to the LORD"—and you forgave the guilt of my sin* (v. 5).

Day 2, read Psalm 51:1-19

Key verse: *Surely I was sinful at birth, sinful from the time my mother conceived me* (v. 5).

Day 3, read Isaiah 6:1-7

Key verse: *"Woe to me!" I cried. "I am ruined! For I am a man of unclean lips, and I live among a people of unclean lips, and my eyes have seen the King, the LORD Almighty"* (v. 5).

Day 4, read Isaiah 64:1-12

Key verse: *All of us have become like one who is unclean, and all our righteous acts are like filthy rags; we all shrivel up like a leaf, and like the wind our sins sweep us away* (v. 6).

Day 5, read Romans 7:14-25

Key verse: *What a wretched man I am! Who will rescue me from this body of death?* (v. 24).

Day 6, read 1 John 1:1 - 2:6

Key verse: *If we claim to be without sin, we deceive ourselves and the truth is not in us* (v. 1:8).

Week 20 Journal

Make notes about your journey with Jesus this week; for example, how He led you; how He spoke to you (see *Your Voice* on page 4); how God worked providentially in your circumstances; breakthroughs and setbacks.

....

....

....

....

Note: there is additional journal space at the end of the guidebook.

Week 21: Our Purpose in Christ

His victory is when we live to fulfill the purpose Jesus has placed in our hearts.

God wants us to succeed on His righteous terms not on our worldly terms. Consequently, as we draw closer to Jesus, the desires of our hearts also draw closer to fulfillment.

David gives us confirmation of this in Psalm 20:4 where he writes: *"May he give you the desires of your heart and make all your plans succeed."*

> The whole thing is nothing extraordinary, nothing special. It has been just a simple surrender, a simple yes to Christ, allowing him to do as he wants. That is why the work is his work. I'm just a little pencil in his hand.
>
> *Mother Teresa* [20]

It may be you have received a calling from the Lord; it may be you sense in your heart that the Lord wants you to be engaged in a particular ministry; it may be you have a deep concern for a group of people who are suffering. Whatever the nature of your desire to serve the Lord, understandably, as you set out on your walk with Him, your focus will be both on accomplishing these desires for His kingdom and your own fulfillment.

But as we proceed along the road of life with Jesus, it seems He is not too interested in us doing what is in our hearts to do; rather, He keeps bringing us back to the present and looking to see how closely we are following Him or going our own way. This frequently leads us to become frustrated with God, and indeed many Christians turn aside at this time, not willing to yield to His gentle hands that are trying to mold us into His likeness. Yet if we are faithful we eventually learn our Lord wants us to live each day for His glory: it is the journey that is important to Him, not the achievement of the goal.

THE PURPOSE OF LIFE

> To live each day,
> where God has placed me,
> for His glory.

But that is not the end to the story, because as we yield fully to Him the desires of our hearts *do* start to become a beautiful reality by His sovereign grace.

Reflections and Questions

Are you able to keep your eyes on the prize of fulfilling God's purpose for your life so that Jesus can say, "Well done good and faithful servant"?

As we approach the end of this guidebook, are you able to see your work as an essential part of your life's purpose in Christ?

Challenge for This Week

As you read the daily Bible passages and spend time with the Lord in prayer this week, ask Him to show you how His purpose for your life and the desires of your heart can be one. If you already know this oneness, pray that you are also one with His way and His timing.

Memory Verse

I pray also that the eyes of your heart may be enlightened in order that you may know the hope to which he has called you, the riches of his glorious inheritance in the saints, and his incomparably great power for us who believe (Ephesians 1:18-19a).

Daily Readings for Week 21

Day 1, read Joshua 1:1-11

Key verse: *"Be strong and very courageous. Be careful to obey all the law my servant Moses gave you; do not turn from it to the right or to the left, that you may be successful wherever you go"* (v. 7).

Day 2, read 2 Samuel 22:26-37

Key verse: *"With your help I can advance against a troop; with my God I can scale a wall"* (v. 30).

Day 3, read Psalm 33:1-22

Key verse: *May your unfailing love rest upon us, O LORD, even as we put our hope in you* (v. 22).

Day 4, read John 17:20-26

Key verse: *[Jesus prayed,] "I have made you known to them, and will continue to make you known in order that the love you have for me may be in them and that I myself may be in them"* (v. 26).

Day 5, read Ephesians 1:15-23

Key verse: *I pray also that the eyes of your heart may be enlightened in order that you may know the hope to which he has called you...* (v. 18a).

Day 6, read Colossians 2:6-12

Key verse: *and you have been given fullness in Christ, who is the head over every power and authority* (v. 10).

Week 21 Journal

Make notes about your journey with Jesus this week; for example, how He led you; how He spoke to you (see *Your Voice* on page 4); how God worked providentially in your circumstances; breakthroughs and setbacks.

Note: there is additional journal space at the end of the guidebook.

Week 22: The Way of Jesus

His victory is when we follow the way of Jesus rather than the way of the world.

Now that we are close to the promised victory, Satan, that great deceiver, will seek to turn us aside: *"Your enemy the devil prowls around like a roaring lion looking for someone to devour"* (1 Peter 5:8b).

The great deceiver's presence will not be obvious to us, because he is the master of deceit; rather he will sow seeds of doubt in our minds. One of these seeds is to show us there are just too many people who follow the way of the world for us to try and continue to follow the way of Jesus Christ. God's victory is not found in great numbers, however, but in great faithfulness.

> So throughout the entire New Testament a sharp line is drawn between the Church and the world. There is no middle ground. The Lord recognizes no good natured "agreeing to disagree" so that the followers of the Lamb may adopt the world's ways and travel along the world's path. The gulf between the true Christian and the world is as great as that which separated the rich man and Lazarus. And, furthermore, it is the same gulf, that is, it is the gulf that divides the world of the ransomed from the world of fallen men.
>
> *A. W. Tozer* [21]

Diary entry February 20th 2003: Today I completed writing *The Battle* that I had started in December 2002. Sometimes the words of these prose come to me as if poured out from heaven; sometimes it takes many weeks or months to wrestle the truth from God's Word by the guidance of His Spirit. *The Battle* is the latter kind, and, indeed, it seems the act of writing it has been a reflection of a battle in the heavenlies against the forces of evil. For, as I rewrote the second part and completed it today with the scriptures inserted, the anguish I had felt all week disappeared even as if the forces of evil had been defeated by the power of God.

THE BATTLE

I desire to do Your will, my Lord, even with all my heart and all my soul and all my mind and all my strength—and yet I so often fail.

Is it just my sinfulness, my Lord?

Or is it the sin of this world that also entices me from Your way?

Or, again, does the power of the evil one also seek to destroy my walk with You?

Often it seems that it is not just one of these evils, but all three battling against Your will for my life. Nevertheless...

With You, my Lord, there is victory over sin.
> *He himself bore our sins in his body on the tree, so that we might die to sins and live for righteousness; by his wounds you have been healed* (1 Peter 2:24).

With You, my Lord, there is victory over the world.
> *"In this world you will have trouble. But take heart! I have overcome the world"* (John 16:33b).

With You, my Lord, there is victory over the evil one.
> *... take up the shield of faith, with which you can extinguish all the flaming arrows of the evil one* (Ephesians 6:16b).

With You, my Lord, victory is assured!

Reflections and Questions

Do you allow the Holy Spirit to work in you so that you are "salt" and "light" at home, at work, and in all life situations?

Have you ever had to choose between the way of Jesus and the way of the world where obedience to Jesus was costly?

Challenge for This Week

As you read the Bible passages this week see how God's way to achieve victory is different to man's way. Also reflect on your journey with our Lord to see if you are trying to face your difficulties and struggles by your own strength and the world's ways, or if you are allowing the Spirit of Christ to work in your life and the situation for His glory.

Memory Verse

Don't you know that friendship with the world is hatred toward God? Anyone that chooses to be a friend of the world becomes an enemy of God (James 4:4b).

Daily Bible Readings for Week 22

Day 1, read Numbers 13:26 to 14:9

Key verse: *If the LORD is pleased with us, he will lead us into that land, a land flowing with milk and honey, and will give it to us* (v. 14:8).

Day 2, read 1 Kings 18:16-39

Key verse: *Then Elijah said to them, "I am the only one of the LORD's prophets left, but Baal has four hundred and fifty prophets"* (v. 22).

Day 3, read 2 Chronicles 20:1-26

Key verse: *"This is what the LORD says to you: 'Do not be afraid or discouraged because of this vast army. For the battle is not yours, but God's'"* (v. 15b).

Day 4, read Ephesians 2:1-10

Key verse: *As for you, you were dead in your transgressions and sins, in which you used to live when you followed the ways of this world and of the ruler of the kingdom of the air, the spirit who is now at work in those who are disobedient* (vv. 1-2).

Day 5, read James 4:1-10

Key verse: *... don't you know that friendship with the world is hatred toward God? Anyone who chooses to be a friend of the world becomes an enemy of God* (v. 4b).

Day 6, read 1 John 2:15-17

Key verse: *Do not love the world or anything in the world. If anyone loves the world, the love of the Father is not in him* (v. 15).

Week 22 Journal

Make notes about your journey with Jesus this week; for example, how He led you; how He spoke to you (see *Your Voice* on page 4); how God worked providentially in your circumstances; breakthroughs and setbacks.

Note: there is additional journal space at the end of the guidebook.

Week 23: Fruit of the Spirit

His victory is when we live daily in His presence with the fruit of the Spirit evident in our lives.

When we are born again, the full measure of the Holy Spirit is immediately available to us. Because our sinful nature is still controlling us, however, the Spirit of God has little room to influence our lives. Therefore, it is only when we *"have crucified the sinful nature with its passions and desires"* that *"love, joy, peace, patience, kindness, goodness, faithfulness, gentleness and self-control"* come to stay (see Galatians 5:22-24).

> Put in its simplest terms, the Bible tells us we need the Spirit to bring fruit into our lives because we cannot produce godliness apart from the Spirit. In our own selves we are filled with all kinds of self-centered and self-seeking desires which are opposed to God's will for our lives. In other words two things need to happen in our lives. First, the sin in our lives needs to be thrust out. Second, the Holy Spirit needs to come in and fill our lives, producing the fruit of the Spirit.
>
> *Billy Graham* [22]

Summer in Abu Dhabi can be unbearable, with temperatures about 120° F and humidity close to 100 percent. Even if the conditions are moderated by a breeze coming off the desert, there is the possibility of a sand storm to add to the miserable climate.

I have been to the United Arab Emirates on many business trips, but this one was particularly arduous, requiring safety inspections of three massive drilling rigs that were under construction. Just to reach the drill floor of these rigs required climbing fourteen flights of stairs in the torrid conditions. The business meetings were also intense, as there were many challenges to keeping a safe working environment in a country that did not have strict safety standards or meaningful consequences for workers being injured.

This trip was a wonderful blessing, however, as the Lord was with me and sustained me by His love and the presence of the fruit of the Spirit. I truly could sing to the Lord!

I SING TO YOU, LORD!

I sing to You, Lord. You give me:
Love over Indifference,
Joy over Misery,
Peace over Turmoil.

I sing to You, Lord. You give me:
Patience over Irritability,
Kindness over Malice,
Goodness over Immorality.

I sing to You, Lord. You give me:
Faithfulness over Fearfulness,
Gentleness over Harshness,
Self-control over Unrestraint.

I sing to You, Lord. You give me:
the fruit of the Spirit over
the fruit of my sinful nature.

I sing to You, Lord!

Reflections and Questions

The Lord did not give us His presence with the fruit of the Spirit only for our own benefit, but also and more importantly, so that our lives may be a witness to draw others to Him. How have you seen this happen in your life including your work life?

Where have you seen the remnants of your worldly nature cause people to be cynical toward the message of our Savior?

Challenge for This Week

Think and pray about how you can now follow Jesus in every detail of your life so that you can be *"the aroma of Christ among those who are being saved and those who are perishing"* (2 Corinthians 2:15).

Memory Verse

But the fruit of the Spirit is love, joy, peace, patience, kindness, goodness, faithfulness, gentleness and self-control (Galatians 5:22-23).

Daily Bible Readings for Week 23

Day 1, read John 4:1-14 and John 7:37-39

Key verse: *"Whoever believes in me, as the Scripture has said, streams of living water will flow from within him"* (v. 7:38).

Day 2, read Acts 2:14-41

Key verse: *Peter replied, "Repent and be baptized, every one of you, in the name of Jesus Christ for the forgiveness of your sins. And you will receive the gift of the Holy Spirit"* (v. 38).

Day 3, read Romans 8:1-17

Key verse: *The mind of sinful man is death, but the mind controlled by the Spirit is life and peace...* (v. 6).

Day 4, read 2 Corinthians 3:7-18

Key verse: *And we, who with unveiled faces all reflect the Lord's glory, are being transformed into his likeness with ever-increasing glory, which comes from the Lord, who is the Spirit* (v. 18).

Day 5, read Ephesians 4:17-32

Key verse: *And do not grieve the Holy Spirit of God, with whom you were sealed for the day of redemption* (v. 30).

Day 6, read 1 Thessalonians 5:12-24

Key verse: *Do not put out the Spirit's fire...* (v. 19, NIV). *Do not quench the Spirit* (v. 19, NASB).

Week 23 Journal

Make notes about your journey with Jesus this week; for example, how He led you; how He spoke to you (see *Your Voice* on page 4); how God worked providentially in your circumstances; breakthroughs and setbacks.

Note: there is additional journal space at the end of the guidebook.

Week 24: Gifts of the Spirit

His victory is when we live daily in His presence with gifts of the Spirit bringing glory to God in our lives.

As we draw close to Jesus, so we gain an understanding of the gifts of the Spirit that God wonderfully brings into our hearts, making each one of us a special part of the body of Christ.

"There are different kinds of gifts, but the same Spirit. ... Now to each one the manifestation of the Spirit is given for the common good" (see 1 Corinthians 12:4 and 7).

When members of a church begin considering spiritual gifts, they sometimes run into difficulty by thinking that God gives them some thing—like an ingredient called administration. No, He doesn't give some thing; He gives Himself. The Gift is a Person. The Holy Spirit equips you with His administrative ability. So His administration begins to become your administration. What you observe when you see a spiritual gift exercised is a manifestation of the Holy Spirit—you see the Holy Spirit equipping and enabling an individual with His abilities and capabilities to accomplish God's work.

Henry T. Blackaby and Claude V. King [23]

As the stresses and strains of the day come upon us it is easy to lose touch with the presence of the Holy Spirit and fall back into our old ways of thinking. To guard against this, I take five minutes or so in the middle of the morning to refocus on the Lord: sometimes in silent prayer at my desk; sometimes picking up my Bible, which I leave by my desk, and reading a short passage of scripture; sometimes reviewing a daily devotional I may have copied to my diary. On this particular day I spent just a few moments in prayer, hoping to lay aside a frustrating incident that had just occurred, and as I did so the Holy Spirit enlightened my mind with these words.

GREAT IS THE LORD!

Great is the Lord and the presence of His Spirit so mighty—

bringing fruit of love, joy, peace, patience, kindness, goodness, faithfulness, gentleness and self-control to each believer;

bringing gifts in many forms, all distributed so that the church, the body of Christ, may be complete.

bringing the grace of God into our lives each moment of the day;

And what does the Lord my God require of me to receive such bounty?

That I love Him:
love Him with all my heart,
love Him with all my soul,
love Him with all my mind, and
love Him with all my strength.

Oh, how great is the Lord!

God gives us His fruit. God gives us His gifts. God gives us His grace. Surely we should rejoice always.

Reflections and Questions

The gifts of the Spirit that are identified in Romans 12:6-8, 1 Corinthians 12:8-10, Ephesians 4:11, and 1 Peter 4:10-11 are summarized below. Identify, as best you can, those gifts that the Lord has given you. Also identify how you are able to use your gifts for the common good.

Apostleship*	Serving	Giving
Prophesy	Encouraging	Faith
Evangelism	Discernment	Healing
Shepherding	Showing Mercy	Miraculous Powers
Teaching	Knowledge	Tongues
Leadership	Wisdom	Interpreting Tongues

* Note: apostleship here is taken to mean today's missionary gift.

Identify other gifts that you think you have:

. . . .

. . . .

Challenge for This Week

As you read the Word of God this week, ask for a clearer understanding of the gifts He is giving you to help build up the body of Christ. Also if you need additional help in understanding the gifts of the Spirit you will find and excellent description in Billy Graham's book, *The Holy Spirit.*[22]

Have you been able to use your gifts of the Spirit in the workplace?

Memory Verse

From him the whole body, joined and held together by every supporting ligament, grows and builds itself up in love, as each part does its work (Ephesians 4:16).

Daily Bible Readings for Week 24

Day 1, read Romans 12:1-8

Key verse: *We have different gifts, according to the grace given us* (v. 6a).

Day 2, read 1 Corinthians 12:1-11

Key verse: *There are different kinds of gifts, but the same Spirit* (v. 4).

Day 3, read 1 Corinthians 12:12-31

Key verse: *For we were all baptized by one Spirit into one body.... Now the body is not made up of one part but of many* (vv. 13a and 14).

Day 4, read Ephesians 4:1-16

Key verse: *From him the whole body, joined and held together by every supporting ligament, grows and builds itself up in love, as each part does its work* (v. 16).

Day 5, read Hebrews 2:1-4

Key verse: *God also testified to it by signs, wonders and various miracles, and gifts of the Holy Spirit distributed according to his will* (v. 4).

<u>Day 6, read 1 Peter 4:1-11</u>

Key verse: *Each one should use whatever gift he has received to serve others, faithfully administering God's grace in its various forms* (v. 10).

Week 24 Journal

Make notes about your journey with Jesus this week; for example, how He led you; how He spoke to you (see *Your Voice* on page 4); how God worked providentially in your circumstances; breakthroughs and setbacks.

Note: there is additional journal space at the end of the guidebook.

Week 25: God's Grace

His victory is when we live daily in His presence and in His abundant grace and power.

It may seem the fruit of the Spirit and the gifts of the Spirit do not in themselves equip us too well for the rigors of daily living. These fruit and gifts, however, are accompanied by the awesome grace and power of God working in the details of our lives as we allow Jesus to be Lord of all. Indeed, it is this awesome grace, which God providentially works in the situations we face, that enables His will to be done through us!

Paul summed this up in His letter to the Romans: *"How much more will those who receive God's abundant provisions of grace and of the gift of righteousness reign in life through the one man, Jesus Christ"* (Romans 5:17b).

> He will give grace, but you must pray for it. He will give grace, but you must search the Scriptures to find it. He will give grace, but you must observe the means He has given. You must get in communion with God and draw near to Him. You must have your times of quiet retirement and still meditation, for although the Lord makes the pipe of His grace flow into the marketplace, yet He expects His people to bring their pitchers there to get them filled. ... He will give grace, but we must go to Him for it in His own appointed way.
>
> *Charles Spurgeon* [24]

In chapter twenty of 2 Chronicles there is a vivid description of a time in the reign of King Jehoshaphat when the Moabites and the Ammonites came with a vast army to war against Judah. The Israelites faced certain defeat, but the LORD promised to be with Jehoshaphat. Then as they set out to meet the invaders, Jehoshaphat stood and said, *"Listen to me, Judah and people of Jerusalem! Have faith in the LORD your God and you will be upheld...."*

Furthermore, Jehoshaphat appointed men to sing to the LORD at the head of the army, and to praise him for the splendor of his holiness saying: "*Give thanks to the LORD, for his love endures forever.*" Then as they began to sing and praise, the Lord set ambushes against the invaders and they were defeated.

This passage teaches us a powerful lesson. Even though a situation may appear hopeless, we are to praise the Lord and trust in Him because He is the omnipotent God who works miracles on our behalf. Therefore, we can live with the peace and joy of the Holy Spirit even as we face insurmountable trials, because His grace can be poured into any situation to fulfill His purpose and bring Him glory.

As an example, when I was facing a difficult trial of being out of work with no doors opening to earn a living, I became fearful of the uncertainty ahead. Nevertheless, the Lord did not allow me to wallow in defeat; rather, He urged me in my spirit to sing praises to Him for the victory that was to come!

REJOICE, REJOICE, REJOICE!

Rejoice, rejoice, rejoice in Jesus our Savior.
Rejoice, rejoice, rejoice in Jesus our Lord.

Though my heart faints within me,
and Your way cannot be seen,
I rejoice in Jesus my Savior,
I rejoice in Jesus my Lord.

It's not my strength that allows this,
but His grace that is poured from above, so
I rejoice in Jesus my Savior,
I rejoice in Jesus my Lord.

Rejoice, rejoice, rejoice in Jesus our Savior.
Rejoice, rejoice, rejoice in Jesus our Lord.

Reflections and Questions

How have you seen the power of God's grace enter into the details of your life?

Have you seen God's providential hand in your work life so that you are more effective in fulfilling your work responsibilities?

Where do you still snuff out this presence of the Holy Spirit, preferring to do things in your own way and your own strength?

Challenge for This Week

One reason we reject the fruit and the power of the Holy Spirit is that we cannot believe God would impart such incredible blessings upon us. Therefore, as you read His Word this week, also pray for the full armor of God (see Ephesians 6:10-18) so you can stand your ground against Satan, the great deceiver, who will want to sow seeds of doubt in your mind for you to discount the blessings Christ so dearly wants to give.

Memory Verse

But he said to me, "My grace is sufficient for you, for my power is made perfect in weakness." Therefore I will boast all the more gladly about my weaknesses, so that Christ's power may rest on me (2 Corinthians 12:9).

Daily Bible Readings for Week 25

Day 1, read Romans 5:12-21

Key verse: *... how much more will those who receive God's abundant provision of grace and of the gift of righteousness reign in life through the one man, Jesus Christ* (v. 17b).

Day 2, read 2 Corinthians 12:1-10

Key verse: *But he said to me, "My grace is sufficient for you, for my power is made perfect in weakness." Therefore, I will boast all the more gladly about my weaknesses, so that Christ's power may rest on me* (v. 9).

Day 3, read 2 Thessalonians 1:3-12

Key verse: *We pray this so that the name of our Lord Jesus may be glorified in you, and you in him, according to the grace of our God and the Lord Jesus Christ* (v. 12).

Day 4, read 1 Timothy 1:12-17

Key verse: *The grace of our Lord was poured out on me abundantly, along with the faith and love that are in Christ Jesus* (v. 14).

Day 5, read 2 Timothy 1:3-14

Key verse: *For the Spirit God gave us does not make us timid, but gives us power, love and self-discipline* (v. 7).

Day 6, read Hebrews 4:14 to 5:10

Key verse: *Let us then approach the throne of grace with confidence, so that we may receive mercy and find grace to help us in our time of need* (v. 16).

Week 25 Journal

Make notes about your journey with Jesus this week; for example, how He led you; how He spoke to you (see *Your Voice* on page 4); how God worked providentially in your circumstances; breakthroughs and setbacks.

Note: there is additional journal space at the end of the guidebook.

Week 26: Go and Make Disciples

By this we witness His love.

This guidebook is about learning to follow Jesus, and just as Jesus said to His disciples two thousand years ago, *"Come, follow me, and I will make you fishers of men"* (Mark 1:17), so He says the same thing to us today.

Here finally is where we must all evaluate the contribution that our life and witness is making to the supreme purpose of him who is the Savior of the world. Are those who have followed us to Christ now leading others to him and teaching them to make disciples like ourselves? Note, it is not enough to rescue the perishing, though this is imperative; nor is it sufficient to build up newborn babes in the faith of Christ, although this too is necessary if the first fruit is to endure; in fact, it is not sufficient just to get them out winning souls, as commendable as this work may be. What really counts in the ultimate perpetuation of our work is the faithfulness with which our converts go out and make leaders out of their converts, not simply more followers.

Robert E. Coleman [25]

In this guidebook I have shared some of the marker stones in my pilgrimage with Jesus, and what an incredible journey that has been and continues to be. Our Savior is also calling you to an incredible journey. Will you follow Him?

WHAT A PILGRIMAGE!

What a pilgrimage with Jesus by our side!
What a pilgrimage with the spirit of self replaced with the Spirit of God!
What a pilgrimage knowing the presence of the living God!
A pilgrimage that starts by being washed by the blood of the Lamb so that we can come openly before the throne of grace!

A pilgrimage that continues by being transformed by the renewing of our minds knowing the awesome presence of God the Father, God the Son and God the Holy Spirit!

A pilgrimage that forms a journey of life for His glory!

Reflections and Questions

Is your life a constant witness of our Savior in word, in deed, and in attitude: to your family, to your friends, to your neighbors, to your work associates, and to others you meet each day?

Identify how you have been able to become more of an *"aroma of Christ among those who are being saved and those who are perishing"* (2 Corinthians 2:15) as you have participated in this guidebook.

Challenge for This Week

As Jesus gains the victory in our lives, He also calls us to go and to make disciples so that His victory may be multiplied.

Memory Verse

Therefore go and make disciples of all nations, baptizing them in the name of the Father and of the Son and of the Holy Spirit, and teaching them to obey everything I have commanded you. And surely I am with you always, to the very end of the age (Matthew 28:19-20).

Daily Bible Readings for Week 26

Day 1, read Matthew 5:13-16

Key verse: *"In the same way, let your light shine before men..."* (v. 16a).

Day 2, read 2 Corinthians 2:12 to 3:6

Key verse: *For we are to God the aroma of Christ among those who are being saved and those who are perishing* (v. 2:15).

Day 3, read 2 Corinthians 4:1-18

Key verse: *It is written: "I believed; therefore I have spoken." With that same spirit of faith we also believe and therefore speak...* (v. 13).

Day 4, read 2 Corinthians 5:11 to 6:2

Key verse: *We are therefore Christ's ambassadors, as though God were making his appeal through us* (v. 5:20a).

Day 5, read Philippians 2:12-18

Key verse: *... so that you may become blameless and pure, children of God without fault in a crooked and depraved generation, in which you shine like stars in the universe as you hold out the word of life...* (vv.15-16a).

Day 6, read 2 Timothy 3:10 to 4:8

Key verse: *Preach the Word; be prepared in season and out of season; correct, rebuke and encourage—with great patience and careful instruction* (v. 4:2).

Week 26 Journal

Make notes about your journey with Jesus this week; for example, how He led you; how He spoke to you (see *Your Voice* on page 4); how God worked providentially in your circumstances; breakthroughs and setbacks.

Note: there is additional journal space at the end of the guidebook.

Conclusion

The following verses from Peter's second letter provide a fitting conclusion to **Following Jesus at Home, at Work, in all of Life**.

His divine power has given us everything we need for a godly life through our knowledge of him who called us by his own glory and goodness. Through these he has given us his very great and precious promises, so that through them you may participate in the divine nature, having escaped the corruption in the world caused by evil desires.

For this very reason, make every effort to…

> *add to your faith goodness;*
>
> *and to goodness, knowledge;*
>
> *and to knowledge, self-control;*
>
> *and to self-control, perseverance;*
>
> *and to perseverance, godliness;*
>
> *and to godliness, mutual affection;*
>
> *and to mutual affection, love.*

For if you possess these qualities in increasing measure, they will keep you from being ineffective and unproductive in your knowledge of our Lord Jesus Christ. But whoever does not have them is nearsighted and blind, forgetting that they have been cleansed from their past sins.

Therefore, my brothers and sisters, make every effort to confirm your calling and election. For if you do these things, you will never stumble, and you will receive a rich welcome into the eternal kingdom of our Lord and Savior Jesus Christ (2 Peter 1:3-11).

You can see in these verses that Peter provides a roadmap to what it means to follow Jesus at home, at work, and in all of life: starting with faith and progressing to agape love. Jesus guides us along the way, but, as Peter notes, we must *make every effort* to follow Him.

Additional Journal Space

Resources

There are a large number of resources on the internet to help Christians make their work life a vital and vibrant part of their walk with Jesus, and, as a natural outflow of this, to engage in workplace ministry. These include:

Resources for all Christians

Christianity 9 to 5,

> http://www.christianity9to5.org/

Institute for Faith, Work & Economics,

> https://tifwe.org/

Theology of Work,

> https://www.theologyofwork.org/

Resources for Business Leaders

C12 Group,

> https://www.c12group.com/

Convene,

> https://www.convenenow.com/

Fellowship of Companies for Christ International,

> https://fcci.org/

Unconventional Business Network

> https://unconventionalbusiness.org/

Endnotes

1. Andrew Murray, *Let Us Draw Nigh* (Fort Washington, PA: Christian Literature Crusade, 1974), 48.

2. John R. W. Stott, *Baptism and Fullness* (Downers Grove IL: InterVarsity Press, 1975), 62.

3. Mother Teresa, *My Life for the Poor* (New York, NY: Ballantine Books, 1987), 91.

4. Dietrich Bonhoeffer, *The Cost of Discipleship* (New York, NY: Macmillan Publishing Co., 1949), 212.

5. Martin Luther, *Sermons of Martin Luther* (Grand Rapids, MI: Baker Book House, 1989, vol. 2), 73.2.

6. Oswald Chambers, *My Utmost For His Highest* (Grand Rapids, MI: Discovery House, 1992), Aug 26th.

7. Billy Graham, *Storm Warning* (Dallas TX: Word Publishing, 1992), 58.

8. Martin Luther, *Sermons of Martin Luther* (Grand Rapids, MI: Baker Book House, 1989, vol. 5), 242.13.

9. Andrew Murray, *The Believer's Prayer Life* (Minneapolis, MN: Bethany House Publishers, 1983), 27.

10. C. S. Lewis, *Mere Christianity* (New York, NY: Macmillan Publishing Company, 1943), 109.

11. Jack W. Hayford, *The Power and the Blessing* (Wheaton, IL: Victor Books, 1994), 181.

12. Doug Sherman and William Hendricks, *Your Work Matters to God* (Colorado Springs, CO: Navpress, 1987).

13. Patrick M. Morley, *Walking with Christ in the Details of Life* (Nashville, TN: Thomas Nelson Publishers, 1992), 237.

14. Max Lucado, *Six Hours One Friday* (Portland, OR: Multnomah, 1989), 161.

15. John R. W. Stott, *The Cross Of Christ* (Downers Grove, IL: InterVarsity Press, 1986), 319.

16. Charles Spurgeon, *Spiritual Warfare in a Believer's Life* (Lynnwood, WA: Emerald Books, 1993), 31.

17. A. W. Tozer, *Christ The Eternal Son* (Camp Hill, PA: Christian Publications, 1991), 43.

18. W. Phillip Keller, *Joshua: Man of Fearless Faith* (Waco, TX: Word Books, 1983), 79.

19. Francis Frangipane, *The Three Battlegrounds* (Cedar Rapids, IA: Arrow Publications, 1989), 8.

20. Mother Teresa, *Total Surrender* (Ann Arbor, MI: Servant Publications, 1985), 139.

21. A. W. Tozer, *The Divine Conquest* (Uhrichsville, OH: Barbour and Company, Inc., 1950), 130.

22. Billy Graham, *The Holy Spirit* (Dallas TX: Word Publishing, 1978), 182.

23. Henry T. Blackaby and Claude V. King , *Experiencing God* (Nashville. TN: LifeWay Press, 1990), 173.

24. Charles Spurgeon, *Grace Abounding in a Believer's Life* (Lynnwood, WA: Emerald Books, 1994), 71.

25. Robert E. Coleman, *The Master Plan of Evangelism* (Grand Rapids, MI: Fleming H. Revell, 1972), 102.

Other Books by Chris J. Fenner

Prayer Awakening: The Privilege & Power of Speaking With God

Chris Fenner's thoughtful book, *Prayer Awakening*, is practical and insightful. He helps the reader deal with real life struggles while offering useful reflections that will guide both the novice and experienced prayer warrior. If you desire to grow in the power of prayer and hearing God's voice you will enjoy this book.

Yes Lord I Will Follow You

The prayers, praises and cries of the heart that are included in *Yes Lord I Will Follow You* have come to Chris over a period of more than thirty years of following Jesus. These will encourage you to seek and find your own glorious journey with Jesus

The Day That God Cried

The heart of *The Day That God Cried* is the story of God's unfolding purpose for America since He created the world; and how He is grieving over our nation as we increasingly deny His living Presence in our culture and even in parts of His church.
Dire as our present circumstances may be, however, the Lord calls us to return to Him through a Spirit-led Awakening.

All books are available at Amazon.com

Contact the Author

www.chrisjfenner.com

cjfenner@comcast.net

281-844-8366

www.ingramcontent.com/pod-product-compliance
Lightning Source LLC
Chambersburg PA
CBHW071002040426
42443CB00007B/631